Theater for Church

Volume 1

24 Quality Scripts for Adult and Youth Drama Teams

David J. Swanson

Swan of Ascent
MEDIA

Theater for Church, Volume 1
Swan of Ascent Media
ISBN-10: 0615569889
ISBN-13: 978-0615569888

Table of Contents

Foreword 3

Acknowledgements 4

Introduction 5

THE CHURCH 8

Acts 2 Community 9

The Pastor Who Does Everything 13

The Fun Squad 18

What Is The Church? 23

IDENTITY 27

Body Image 28

Suicide 32

Personal Computer 35

Signs of Change 40

Family Feud 44

CHRISTIAN LIVING 51

Dead or Alive 52

Christian Robot Replacement 58

No Complaints 65

Love Language 70

Catwalk of Shame 75

Discipleship 80

GOD'S CHARACTER: 83

Magic Answers 84

I Don't Buy It 89

Dueling Detectives 93

PRAYER 98

Prayer Warrior 99

Three Different Prayers 102

REACHING OUT 106

For Want of a Sandwich 107

Coins or the Pile 112

CHRISTMAS 119

Down to Earth 120

Foreword

I am incredibly blessed to have David Swanson as part of the 'volunteer staff' with our youth ministry. He has served as the Drama Director for several years at our church. We have been in partnership for the past few years and God has used him to train and equip actors, to write scripts, and to move audiences forward in their own discipleship process.

An element of drama is one of the most impacting ways of communication that I have had the opportunity to experience. It draws an audience in, captivates their attention, and moves their heart. For the past several years, David Swanson has written scripts that allow for this captivation of the heart and mind, moving people toward following Jesus all the while partnering with the sermon and message of the program. In our youth ministry, we have used drama as a way to illustrate the message and make people think about the message. We have seen students respond with hearts and minds that are willing to do something different, to change. The Spirit of God has used the scripts in great ways in the discipleship process and journey with teenagers and people at West E. Free Church.

I am convinced that if you are able to implement some of the scripts found in the following pages in your ministry, in your sphere of influence, and in your own life, God will use that script to challenge and move you to a deeper, more profound and prolific relationship with him.

-Pastor Chris Rollman
West Evangelical Free Church
Wichita, Kansas

Acknowledgements

There have been an innumerable amount of people who have helped make this book a reality. I say "innumerable" because I've never really been good at counting. On the short list of people who absolutely must be thanked you will find:

- Laura, who gave me a chance to direct, even though I was completely inexperienced.
- Pastor Ken, who supported drama in the church long before it was popular.
- Pastor Greg, Pastor Chris, and DA Horton for their guidance, support and contributions to this book.
- Nathan, Jill, Stacy, Wes, PJ, Carrie, and the rest of the assistant directors who have given time to directing these sketches over the years.
- Chris, who makes our adult drama sparkle on stage.
- Sally, for the photography which graces the cover of this book.
- Carol, for her inscrutatious (not a word) copyediting skills.
- Eric, Bri, Ben, Susan, Emily, Stephanie, Austin, DJ, Aaron, Chris, Samm, Crystal, Ashley, PJ, Joy, Sally, Lauren, Jordan, Jeffrey, Matt, Katlyn, Levi, David, Tyler, Jennifer, Ana, Bethany, Maddie, Hunter, Michelle and the rest of the drama kids, past and present, at WEFC. Without you, drama would just be a grown man playing with costumes and writing down conversations that only happen in his head.
- And above all, my darling wife Carrie, who is my first proofreader, encourager, idea tester, and a pretty handy assistant director herself.

Thank you all for allowing God to use you as we created theater for church.

Introduction

<u>Why Drama?</u>
You leaf through the pages of the New Testament and, try as you might, you can't seem to find any examples of Jesus putting on a play for his followers. There don't seem to be any examples of the early church doing sketches before they speak and, though the Greeks had been performing theater for 500 years prior to the coming of Christ, there isn't even a mention of Greek theater in the Bible.

So why are you so interested in worshipping God through drama?

God is a theatrical God. For a great discussion on the differences between theater and drama, I'll refer you to <u>The Playwright's Guidebook</u> by Stuart Spencer. Suffice it to say that theater is all around us. When a man proposes to his girlfriend on a stadium scoreboard, that's theater. When a young boy does a cartwheel for his mom, that's theater.

God works theatrically. Rending the veil in the temple at the moment of Christ's death is theater. It was set in motion, building the drama and significance over thousands of years, and at the key moment the veil is torn leading us to a larger truth: namely that with Christ there is no longer a barrier between us and God.

Okay, fine. But what about drama, specifically? Sketches and the like?

Look at the way Christ taught. He often spoke in parables. Fictional stories designed to illustrate a greater point. In fact, in some cases he spoke only in parables, refusing to explain their meaning as we see in Mark 4. This method of teaching, bringing illustrations to a dramatic presentation, is effective for bringing a lesson to a large group of people. If confusion is the first step to learning, then leaving an audience wondering what a parable means may be the first step to understanding biblical truth.

Yeah, but why is Christian drama so awful sometimes?

The only thing worse than no drama is bad drama. This is a mantra I often repeat to my drama teams and it's one that a church looking to engage their congregation through theater should keep in mind.

Bad drama is often a confusing mix of allegory and melodrama and leaves the audience feeling abused. Just because a dramatist wants an audience to believe a credo doesn't mean a character needs to explicitly state it. All too often scripts written for the church involve Person A being a comical but ignorant heathen and Person B explaining gospel truth to them in the form of quoted scripture and witty one-liners.

This is drama abuse. It is the equivalent of Frodo Baggins, the intrepid protagonist from the epic *Lord of the Rings* films, turning to the camera on the steps of Mount Doom after finally ridding himself of the One Ring and saying "See kids? This is why you should stay away from addictive substances like drugs and alcohol."

Sketches versus Skits
Another reason drama can be so uncomfortable to watch in the church is because drama teams are putting on skits instead of sketches. What's the difference? A skit is what you do around the campfire. The characters are one-dimensional and often are stereotypes. They serve as stick figures to carry out a gag, whereas a sketch is a miniature play. The characters have backgrounds, subtext, secret desires, and inner motivations. They are complex. A sketch draws the audience into the scene as a movie, novel or play does. The audience suspends their disbelief and understands the drama experientially. Perform sketches, not skits.

Help on Building your Drama Team
This introduction is not a treatise on everything you need to know about drama in the church. I'd refer you to the seminal work Drama Ministry by Steve Pederson, Zondervan, for a good primer on building your drama team. He also delves into what makes drama work in a church and what drama does best.

Producing These Sketches
The sketches in this book were written in conjunction with a message delivered in the church. They are not stand alone messages in and of themselves. It is up to the pastor to do the preaching, as that is his strength. The drama brings the audience in, asks questions, and sets the expectation that the questions will be answered directly by the Word of God.

Implementing these sketches can be as easy or as difficult as you choose. Some are monologues set in what I call "The Testimonial Nowhere". It is a blank stage offering no clues as to setting, some are full costume dramas, and others require a great number of people. No matter what script you choose, the important thing to remember is that your audience is educated in the science of theater. Their expectations for good theater are high so your drive for excellence should be comparably high. God deserves your best.

Using This Book
All of the sketches in this book were performed at West Evangelical Free Church in front of a live audience. Each sketch has an introduction which includes such information as The Point of the sketch, Biblical References, Setting, Cast, Tech Needs including sound effects, lighting, props and costumes, and a personal note from me about each script. With this context, I hope that you'll find the same success in reaching your congregation that we did during the original performances.

There are several places in this book where a pop culture reference or regional reference is included that may not fit with your culture or location. Those items are denoted like this. When you come across something like this, feel free to change it to something that makes more sense to your audience. These are the only parts of the scripts you are legally permitted to change.

Copyrights, Performance Rights, and Royalties

In the last decade or so, people have become much more aware of intellectual property rights and copyright infringement. Whether it is music downloads, movies, or books, people are learning that if they didn't create it, they don't own it, and thus they can't copy it.

I, as playwright, am giving you permission to photocopy the scripts in this book to hand to your actors and technical crew for a given production. Once the production is complete, I ask that you destroy the photocopies. If another organization wants to do the same sketch, please direct them to wherever they can purchase a copy of this book. You will sleep soundly knowing that you're helping support a Christian artist and have eschewed the life of a pirate.

Performances of the sketches contained herein may be performed royalty free and without express written consent provided the performers or sponsoring organization have purchased a copy of this book.

The author may be contacted at: SwanofAscent@gmail.com.

Benediction
May God richly bless you and your craft. May the Holy Spirit use these sketches to His glory.

~David J. Swanson

The Church

If we are the body...

Acts 2 Community

David J. Swanson

The Point:

> There are some things about the Christian life that are just flat out un-American. Really. The idea that we should be self-sufficient, relying on ourselves alone leaves no room for dependence on God. The idea that others in need are in need because they didn't perform well enough flies in the face of Jesus' command to love one another and to look after widows and orphans. Acts 2 gives us an example of what our church should look like.

Biblical Reference:

> Acts 2, Acts 4:32-34

Setting:

> The testimonial nowhere: A non-descript bare stage.

Cast:

> ACTOR 1: Self-righteous American.
> ACTOR 2: Self-righteous American.
> ACTOR 3: Self-righteous American.
> ACTOR 4: Self-righteous American.
> ACTOR 5: A friend in need.

Tech needs:

> Dramatic spot lights. Perhaps stools for some of the ACTORS to sit on.

Playwright Notes:

> Position the four actors together, looking out at the audience as if it were a four-person monologue. When ACTOR 5 enters, feel free to treat ACTORS 1-4 like a Greek chorus, thinking and reacting in unison. Make sure the last blackout is quick to give the last line a little extra zip.

Four actors are on stage. They speak dramatically, in pretentious tones. The word "I" gets longer and more emphasized the more they say it.

ACTOR 1:   I am an American

ACTOR 2:   American ends in "I can"

ACTOR 3:   I can do anything I put my mind to

ACTOR 4:   I can be anything I want to be

ACTOR 2:   If I work hard enough

ACTOR 4:   If I study long enough

ACTOR 3:   If I do what I'm told

ACTOR 1:   I can be anyone I want.

Pause

ACTOR 2:   The future is what I make of it.

ACTOR 3:   The future is there for the taking-

ACTOR 4:   -if I'm willing to take it.

ACTOR 1:   God is my copilot-

ACTOR 3:   -helping me get what I want.

Pause

ACTOR 4:   I am an American

ACTOR 2:   I am strong

ACTOR 3:   I am smart

ACTOR 1:   I am powerful

ACTOR 4:   I am brilliant

ACTOR 2:   I am deserving

ACTOR 3:   I am entitled

5 enters. 5 speaks in normal conversational tones.

ACTOR 5: I need some help.

ACTORS 1,2,3,4: *(aghast)* What?

ACTOR 5: I need help.

ACTOR 1: I.... can't hear you.

ACTOR 2: I.... am busy.

ACTOR 3: I won't be slowed down by your weakness.

ACTOR 5: But, I can't do this on my own.

ACTOR 1: I am important

ACTOR 4: -to my church

ACTOR 3: -to my family

ACTOR 2: -to myself

ACTOR 1: I can't be soiled by your dirt

ACTOR 3: *(venomously)* I can't be tainted by your neediness

ACTOR 4: I will help you.

ACTORS 1, 2, and 3 gasp

       If... it makes me look good

ACTOR 3: If it makes me feel good.

ACTOR 2: If it makes me a better person.

ACTOR 5: I'm not a charity case. I just need a hand.

ACTOR 4: To do what?

ACTOR 5: Build a community

ACTOR 1: A what?

ACTOR 5: A community.

ACTORS 1,2, and 3 speak overlapping one another. They hang on the word 'I'.

ACTOR 1: Well, I.... I...

ACTOR 2: I should say I... I...

ACTOR 3: Um, I... I...

ACTOR 5: It's not an "I"... It's a "we".

ACTOR 4:   A we?

ACTOR 5:   An us. A community.

ACTOR 1:   I... think this person is afflicted.

ACTOR 5:   Who is the church?

ACTOR 3:   We are.

ACTOR 5:   Who is here to love those who don't know Christ?

ACTOR 2:   We are.

ACTOR 5:   Who does the Holy Spirit empower?

ACTOR 4:   Us.

ACTOR 5:   It's a community. We. Together. Us.

ACTOR 1:   But American doesn't end in "us".

ACTOR 5:   No, but do you know what does? Glorious.

Blackout

The Pastor Who Does Everything

David J. Swanson

The Point:

A pastor can't do the entire ministry in a church. Each member of the church needs to do his part.

Biblical Reference:

Luke 10:2, Matthew 10:37-39

Setting:

A church on a Saturday afternoon.

Cast:

PASTOR: Preferably, one of the church's existing pastors.
BRIDE: A woman in a wedding gown
GROOM: A man in a tuxedo or dark suit
COUPLE: Young couple.

Tech needs:

Wedding Dress, Tux or dark suit, chair, oily clothes for PASTOR, working cell phone, beeping watch.

Playwright Notes:

This hilarious sketch was used to kick off our annual ministry drive that asks our congregation to find out where God would have them serve for the year. The PASTOR was our adult ministries pastor who played the frenzied, overwhelmed pastor with great familiarity. Perhaps that's why he commissioned this sketch.

Lights up. Pastor is on stage. A young couple is down center dressed for their wedding day.

PASTOR: Dearly beloved, we are gathered here today to celebrate a joyous union of souls. Marriage is a gift from God, and a covenant one should not enter lightly. Before I go much farther, I should apologize for my appearance. You see I was changing the oil on the church van a few minutes ago and I had forgotten to drain the oil before I removed the filter. Oil everywhere. Anyway, my tux was completely ruined, and so here I am.

Watch beeps.

PASTOR: Shoot. Um... Let's all pray silently about the meaning of marriage. *(Steps stage right. Talks stage right to invisible Bible study.)* Sorry about that. I want to thank you all for coming to our Bible study as we continue our walk through Leviticus. I also wanted to remind you that for those of you interested in going with me on our missions trip to Jamaica, applications are due to me by next Friday.

Watch beeps.

PASTOR: Oh sorry. I've just got so much going on. Tell you what. Let's pray silently about the meaning of the word "Leviticus". OK? *(Steps stage left. Talks stage left to invisible choir.)* Hi. Thank you all for coming. I appreciate your patience. It's great to see all of you budding singers. Who knew the Church was so blessed? I know we haven't had a choir in a while, but I think this choir is going to surprise a lot of people. Let's start at measure 44 and let's work on the chorus. Ready,

(Waves hands. Sings "Joyful, joyful we adore thee". Continues to wave hands as he addresses center audience.)

PASTOR: Who gives this woman to be the bride? You? Great. Oh guys, why don't you go light your unity candle thingy and I'll be right with you. *(PASTOR steps stage right. Talks stage right. Occasionally waves hands to direct "choir".)*

Now, as we have seen, Leviticus is more than a book about rules or law. We've seen the guilt offering, the grain offering, the burnt offering, and my personal favorite, the wave offering. *(Waves and smiles).*

COUPLE knocks at the door off stage.

PASTOR: If you'll excuse me.

Opens door.

PASTOR: Come in.

A young couple is at the door. They see the audience and react.

PASTOR: Hey guys. Come in. No, it's fine.

The couple enters and sits on a couple of chairs upstage left, obviously uncomfortable because of the audience.

PASTOR: So, how many days until the big day?

They answer in mime.

PASTOR: Cool. Well you've been doing great on your pre-marital counseling. Your compatibility tests came back. We learned a lot from that, especially about you, Mike.

Laughs. The couple looks more and more agitated.

PASTOR: The only thing we have left to cover is the wedding night.

The COUPLE quickly get up and leave through the door they came in.

PASTOR: No? Okay, another time then.

Cell phone rings. Pastor answers it while he continues to direct the "choir".

PASTOR: Hello? Yes. No, it's not a bad time, what's on your mind? Uh-huh. Uh-huh.

PASTOR Returns center stage. Covers mouth piece.

PASTOR: *(Whispers)* Do you take him to be your husband?

(Back on phone) Uh, huh sure. Oh, absolutely.

(Covers mouthpiece again.) and do you take this lady to be your wife?

(Before groom can answer Pastor holds up his finger.)

Yeah? Okay, hold on. Let me write that down.

(Turns GROOM around so PASTOR can write on his back.)

PASTOR: Thursday 10:00pm. Yeah, I've got time. I'm usually busy until midnight, every day, but Thursday is my off day. I'm only busy until 9. Okay, see you then.

Hangs up phone.

PASTOR: So where were we?

BRIDE runs off crying. Pastor shrugs his shoulders.

PASTOR: *(To GROOM)*

Since you're free now, would you mind helping me paint the activity center? I've got to get it finished before youth group tonight.

GROOM leaves in a huff. Phone rings. Pastor starts to look a little annoyed.

PASTOR: *(Agitated)* Hello? Yes, dear… No, there isn't anyone else…. Because I'm covering the nursery. Um, I think we've got seven in there now… Seven…. I'm sure they're fine. They were all asleep a few hours ago…. Fine, I'll go check on them.

Hangs up.

PASTOR: Ok, sorry everyone. I have to go check on the nursery. My wife seems to think it's unwise to leave seven babies alone in a room for more than a few hours. I'll be right back, though, and we'll get this Bible study/wedding/choir practice finished up. MmmKay? Thanks for your understanding.

(Exits center aisle.)

Blackout

The Fun Squad

David J. Swanson

The Point:

> Everyone is gifted with something that God expects us to use to His glory, and everyone is needed in their capacity. There is no such thing as an extra member of the church, an unneeded part of the team, or a superfluous part of the body.

Biblical Reference:

> 1 Corinthians 12, Romans 12:6-8

Setting:

> A pre-school classroom or auditorium. The audience is 4 and 5 year olds.

Cast:

TEACHER:	Optional, but this sets the stage for the Fun Squad and helps establish the audience as small children.
C-	The smart one. The leader of The Fun Squad
H- R, I, S-	Dull witted followers. Performers in The Fun Squad.

> C.H,R,I,S all wear matching shirts with their letters on their chests.

Tech Needs:

> Five matching shirts with letters on them. A handheld mic for the TEACHER.

Playwright Notes:

> This was one of our best loved sketches of the year. The sketch works the same way Laurel and Hardy, or the Marx Brothers worked all those years ago. One smart one and the rest are lovable idiots.

Lights up.

TEACHER enters and takes center stage, talking to the audience as if they were 4 year olds.

TEACHER: All right boys and girls. If you sit nice and quietly, we will have a very special presentation. Billy, stop throwing spitballs. Yes, you Mister. *(Improv getting control of the class).* I've arranged with Principal Chris, to bring you something I'm sure you'll all love. Okay, Please welcome our guests "The Fun Squad!"

C, H, R, I, S enter clapping a fun cadence. They are turned around so you cannot see the front of their shirts.

C: *(turns around. He has a "C" on his shirt).*
Well, good evening kids. We're The Fun Squad. Are you ready to have some fun? Well, we're here to tell you about the funnest thing in the whole wide world. You know what that is? It's the saving power of Jesus C!

H: *(turns around)* H!

R: *(turns around)* R!

I: *(turns around)* I!

S: *(turns around. Said with leading inflection.)* S!

Long pause. They smile compulsively. The squad looks at each other.

C: Um. Where's Eddie?

H: Eddie?

C: Yeah, Eddie. Where is he?

R:	Oh, he said he wasn't going to make it tonight.
C:	What!?
I:	Yeah, he said he had too much homework and then he really wanted to finish Red Faction.
C:	Red Faction?
S:	It's a game.
I:	For XBOX
C:	I know it's a game. Why is he playing that instead of being here?
H:	He figured we had enough people.
C:	What?
R:	Five out of six ain't bad.
I:	Yeah, what's the problem?
C:	Are you kidding me?
I:	Um. No.
C:	Look at what we spell.

H, R, I, and S, look at their shirts

H:	Our shirts say "Chris"
I:	Who's Jesus Chris?
C:	Exactly. Now do you see our problem?

Long pause as H, R, I, S figure it out.

H,R,I,S:	Ohhhhhhh.
S:	I wish Eddie were here.
H:	Never mind Eddie, what do we do?
C:	Do? The whole show is ruined!
I:	We can improvise.
H:	Improvise, how?
I:	Follow my lead.
C:	Oh boy.

I: Hi kids! We're here to tell you about.... *(Organizes team to say HIS RC).* HIS RC!

C: What's that mean?

I: It means, kids, His.. Radio Control, of course. Like an airplane!

C: No, no, no!

I: What?

C: That doesn't even make any sense.

S: Okay, I've got it. *(organizes team to say RICHS).* We're here to talk to you kids about investing, mutual funds, and 401(k)s to realize all the RICHS you can have.

C: What are you talking about? They're four years old.

S: Never too early to start saving.

C: This is hopeless.

R: I have a great idea

C: I doubt it.

R: Here. (Organizes team to say I CRHS)

C: What's that mean?

R: I don't know. I just felt like rearranging the letters.

H: Forget it. Let's just go with "Chris".

I: Who's Chris?

H: Their principal. Let's just get through this and get out of this.

C: Fine. *(they arrange back into CHRIS order).* Hey kids! We're here to tell you about the, uh, amazing speaking powers of C

H: H

R: R

I: I

S: S

C: Je-um, Principal

ALL:	CHRIS! *(S says "Christ" by mistake)*
H:	And he's looking to come into your heart – er, um house, to have coffee.
C:	Coffee?
H:	Go with it.
R:	And Principal Chris is the only one that can take your sins, um, stains away.
C:	Stains?
R:	When he uses carpet cleaner on those nasty stains.
I:	And Principal Chris died on the cross to pay for your, um.... No, no, boys and girls. Principal Chris isn't dead. No No, shhhhh.
C:	Forget this. You guys are on your own. (exits)
S:	Now what do we do?
H:	Call Eddie and tell him he ruined our show.
I:	Good idea. (They exit)

Blackout

What Is The Church?

David J. Swanson

The Point:

The church is what we build it to be. We are the church.

Biblical Reference:

Ephesians 5:15-21, Ephesians 2:20, Matthew 18:16-20

Setting:

Three actors center stage. Two sitting in folding chairs. No other staging. This sketch was performed by starting a worship song towards the end and then building into the song, so the band was already on stage, but in darkness, when the sketch started.

Cast:

Three people of any type. Varied dress preferred.

Tech needs:

Dramatic light, preferably accented from behind. This sketch goes right into a song from the band so you'll have to transition sound and lights to the worship band.

Playwright Notes:

This sketch is more like a monologue than a sketch. The three actors address the audience directly, first with questions, then with answers. It is an anthem, a call to arms, a manifesto.

Dramatically speaking, it works best if the first lines are played with a very low energy and slow pacing. This leaves the actors plenty of room to build the intensity as the sketch develops.

Two actors sit in folding chairs placed center stage at a 90 degree angle but facing away from each other. A third actor stands behind them. The three give an air of togetherness but disunity. They are pondering the same question but in different ways.

Lights up. Lights are simple, yet dramatic here and build later.

ACTOR 1:   Is it true? What they say about the church? Is it true that the church is dying? Irrelevant?

ACTOR 2:   Is it a bastion of intolerance like they say?

ACTOR 3:   A house of hate? A place where holier-than-thou types go to feel superior?

ACTOR 1:   A place of judgment? A place of guilt? Is it true?
(Beat)
If not, then what is the church?

ACTOR 2:   *(Stands)*
Is it a country club, designed to make sure we see our friends every week? A social group of politically similar, economically similar, skin-color similar that meet to pat each other on the back. Is that the church?

ACTOR 3:   *(Stands)*
Is it soaring gothic architecture? Stained glass? Pipe organs? Wide stages? Flashing lights? Pumping sound systems? Contemporary rock with vaguely Christian lyrics sung with arms raised because that looks good? Is that the church?

ACTOR 1:   Is it indoctrination?

ACTOR 2:   Supplication?

ACTOR 3:   Self-adoration?

ACTOR 2:   Endless salutations?

    (Beat)

    Is it?

    (Pause)

ACTOR 1:   I am the church. *(2 and 3 overlapping)*

ACTOR 2:   I am the church.

ACTOR 3:   I am the church.

A build in energy begins. Worship band starts to play the song that will build through the rest of the sketch.

ACTOR 1:   When two or three are gathered in His name, we are the church.

ACTOR 2:   When I show the love of Christ to my brothers and sisters, I am the church.

ACTOR 3:   When I reach out to someone in need, I am the church.

ACTOR 1:   *(grabs chair, steps up on it during line)*

    We are the bricks of the church, laid side by side, built on the backs of the apostles, with Jesus Christ as our cornerstone. We are the church.

Lights change to echo the build in energy.

ACTOR 2:   When we are filled with the Holy Spirit, singing psalms and hymns, making music to the Lord in our hearts, arms raised, voices crying out, we are the church!

These lines fall with no break between them, as if spoken with a single voice.

ACTOR 1:   *(Intense)* I am the church!

ACTOR 2:   I will not be a fool!

ACTOR 3:   I will not be thoughtless!

ACTOR 1:   I will not hate!

ACTOR 3:   I will not posture and pretend!

ACTOR 2: I will not make church about me!

ACTOR 1: I will be real,

ACTOR 2: Be honest,

ACTOR 3: Be vulnerable.

ACTOR 1: I will be me.

ACTOR 2: We are the bride of Christ.

ACTOR 3: We are His people.

ACTOR 1: We are the church.

Band builds into song. Lights off on actors, up on band. Actors can either leave the stage or join in worship.

Identity

And you are...?

Body Image

David J. Swanson

The Point:

Sometimes we wear a mask of perfection, but other times we wear a mask of insecurity, talking ourselves out of what we want. Self confidence can be severely undermined by a poor body image.

Biblical Reference:

Proverbs 4:23-27, 1 John 4:16-18, Romans 5:6-8, 1 John 4:9-11

Setting:

A girl sitting at a table at lunch in school. Around her three actors portraying physical manifestations of her own self-doubt.

Cast:

PMOHOSD 1, 2, 3: Three women who hover around her like a thought bubble. They are Physical Manifestations of Her Own Self-Doubt (PMOSHOSD). They act as one, representing, not her conscience, but what she says about herself.

CRYSTAL: A high school girl. Thin and attractive, but short. Her low self-esteem is her downfall.

JARED: A high school guy. Athletic, though likable and not intimidating.

DAEDRA: A platonic friend of JARED's either male or female. She's aware of JARED's interest in CRYSTAL.

Tech Needs:

A lunch table, lunch tray with lunch. A few chairs. A brown bagged lunch.

Playwright Notes:

This sketch was part of our "Masks" series that looked at the masks we wear in our life. A poor body image, or needlessly dwelling on one's perceived flaws can be detrimental to our ability to relate to others and to do God's will. Bulimia and Anorexia are obvious extreme consequences of poor body image, but there are other less serious consequences that keep us from our potential and damage our relationships.

Lights up. CRYSTAL enters holding lunch tray with PMOHOSD 1, 2, and 3 hovering closely behind her in a diamond formation. CRYSTAL walks to a lunch table, stops, cranes her neck on her tip-toes and scans the lunchroom looking for a friend. PMOHOSD 1, 2, and 3 scan the room with her in a synchronized fashion. Resigned to the empty lunch table, CRYSTAL plops into a chair.

PMOHOSD 1: Why did God make us so short?

PMOHOSD 2: Seriously, it's a problem.

PMOHOSD 3: We pretty much need to wear heels just to keep people from patting us on the head when they walk by.

PMOHOSD 1: It's embarrassing.

PMOHOSD 3: We're not a child. We're a 17 year old teenager.

PMOHOSD 2: Maybe if we carried a little ladder around with us wherever we went.

PMOHOSD 1: That's a stupid idea. Where are we going to hide a ladder?

PMOHOSD 2: It was just a suggestion.

PMOHOSD 3: It wouldn't be so bad if God hadn't made us so fat.

PMOHOSD 2: No kidding. Two words for us. Chunky. Monkey.

PMOHOSD 3: No wonder no one will sit with us at lunch.

PMOHOSD 1: We look like a bowling ball with an orange stuck on top.

PMOHOSD 2: Hey we're in shape. Round is a shape.

PMOHOSD 3: I can't believe we took all this food. An apple AND a yogurt? We shouldn't be eating this.

PMOHOSD 1: Not if we want friends.

PMOHOSD 3: Not if we want JARED Thompson to notice us.

PMOHOSD 2: Speaking of which, holy cow, he's coming over here!

PMOHOSD 1: He is? But we're sitting by ourselves! We look like a loser!

PMOHOSD 3: I hope he doesn't see us!

JARED enters.

JARED: Hi, Crystal.

PMOHOSD 3: Crap.

CRYSTAL: Hi, Jared.

JARED: I noticed you were sitting here by yourself.

PMOHOSD 1: Quick, make something up!

CRYSTAL: Oh, my friends are all in the bathroom. They're coming.

JARED: They are? Oh, okay.

PMOHOSD 2: He looks annoyed. What did we do to annoy him?

PMOHOSD 1: Quick change the subject.

PMOHOSD 3: Remember to smile.

PMOHOSD 1: But not too much. Our teeth are kinda yellow today.

PMOHOSD 2: And don't stand up. We're short, remember?

CRYSTAL: Um. Uh. Are you going to the football game tonight?

JARED: Football game? Uh. Yeah. I'm on the team, remember?

PMOHOSD 1,2, and 3 pound their heads in unison.

PMOHOSD 3: Stupid, stupid, stupid.

CRYSTAL: Oh, yeah. Well, um. Good luck on the game. Hope you win.

PMOHOSD 1: *(Notices stain on shirt. Crystal also notices stain on her shirt.)* Oh my gosh! We have a stain on our shirt.

PMOHOSD 3: A stain! Where?

PMOHOSD 1: On our collar. Why can't we wear clean clothes?

PMOHOSD 2: This is a nightmare. It's bad enough we have to wear these hand-me downs.

PMOHOSD 1: We need to get out of here before he notices.

CRYSTAL: Well, I'm going to the library for the rest of lunch.

JARED: Right. Okay. Later.

PMOHOSD 2: Go, go, go. But don't look like we're hurrying.

PMOHOSD 1: Cover the stain.

PMOHOSD 3: Don't smile too much.

PMOHOSD 2: Walk like we're tall.

PMOHOSD 1: And skinny.

PMOHOSD 2: Just don't look back.

PMOHOSD 3: This is the worst day of our life.

They exit. Jared sits dejectedly. DAEDRA enters.

DAEDRA: Hey, I saw you finally got up the nerve to talk to Crystal. So? How'd it go?

JARED: Eh, she blew me off. She's definitely not into me. The whole time we were talking it was like she was thinking about someone else.

Blackout

Suicide

David J. Swanson

The Point:

Those who are left behind after a suicide face a number of questions. Among those questions will be wondering if they ever told the deceased about the power of Jesus.

Biblical Reference:

Genesis 1:27; 2 Corinthians 5:19; Psalm 139:13; 1 Corinthians 10:13

Setting:

Two actors give overlapping monologues, addressing the audience directly.

Cast:

TYLER: A teenager. A friend of Eric's. His reaction to Eric's suicide is anger, both at Eric and at himself.

KATLYN: A teenage platonic friend of Eric's. Her reaction to Eric's suicide is to grieve.

Tech needs:

Simple lighting. Black stage. Katlyn can start on a stool.

Playwright Notes:

Two friends talking about a friend of theirs that took his own life. They sit on opposite sides of the stage. The actors speak slowly as if in a confessional booth. They are unaware of each other and deliver their lines like two intertwined monologues. The actors' speech is slow and distracted. There is a torrent of conflicting thoughts and memories in the subtext.

As both actors react emotionally at the same time, balance Katlyn's teary-eye grief with Tyler's anger. One soft, one loud.

Lights up.

TYLER: Why is it that we only think about the important things after they're gone? Why don't we realize what we have when we have it?

KATLYN: Eric was 17 when he… He was my friend. Well, I thought we were friends. We would hang out every so often. He was quiet in a big group, but like when you got to spend time with just him, he would come out of his shell.

TYLER: Eric had this thing he would do. It's stupid, but it made me laugh. He could flip his eyelids inside out. Then he'd go around with this creepy voice, like "Acchchch, I'm coming for you." He would do this to random people in the mall. It was hilarious. Creepy, but hilarious.

KATLYN: He had a dark sense of humor, but that was the thing with Eric. He could laugh at anything it seemed.

TYLER: I remember when his parents split up. I thought it would hit him hard, but he just laughed and said "Hey, I get two Christmases!" That was Eric. He could joke about anything.

KATLYN: I couldn't believe it when Jessica told me. I thought she was making a stupid joke. But she was crying. It wasn't a joke.

TYLER: *(Begins to get angry.)*
He didn't even leave a note. How can you do that and not leave a note? Let us know why. Tell us what you were thinking!

KATLYN: *(Begins to get teary-eyed)*
What was he thinking? I don't know. We had plans to play the new on that Saturday. He was super pumped about it. But then Friday night, I guess he'd had enough.

TYLER: Of what? High School? Are you kidding me, Eric? You couldn't handle High School? There's so much more out there, so much more we were going to do---

KATLYN: It's weird, seeing his facebook page. His mom doesn't know his password, and facebook won't take it down. So it just sits there. I don't have the heart to unfriend him. There he is, smiling in that stupid picture I took on my cell phone. This grainy picture of this kid with a huge sombrero on, just… laughing. But he's gone…
(Silence)
People leave messages to him on his wall. Do they think he's going to read them? I don't think the first thing he did when he got to heaven was check his facebook page.

TYLER: I think he went to heaven. I hope. I guess, I don't really know. We never really talked about stuff like that.

KATLYN: Eric and I never really talked about a lot of things that mattered, I guess.

Slow fade to Blackout

Personal Computer

David J. Swanson

The Point:

> The Christian life is one of controlling what we put into our life and into our minds. What goes in, eventually comes out. Garbage in begets garbage out. More practically speaking, if we fill our lives with selfish thoughts, sinful media, and unloving thought, then we can't very well expect the love of Christ to shine through to others.

Biblical Reference:

> Colossians 3:2, Philippians 3:19-20, Matthew 16:23

Setting:

> The office at a bank or credit union used to finalize car loans.

Cast:

> KAREN: 16 year old high school girl. Sweet and petite.
> LOAN OFFICER: Cordial loan officer lacking some common sense.

Tech needs:

> A desk, a computer, a cup with pens, a lamp, two chairs, some paperwork to make the desk look lived in. LOAN OFFICER needs a shirt and tie.

Playwright Notes:

> This sketch relies on the complete impossibility of KAREN being anything other than a nice, polite young woman. The more cordial the two characters are to each other in the beginning, the funnier the sketch will be as the LOAN OFFICER quietly passes judgment on her for her supposed exploits and stops listening to her. The criminal history at the end should be read as one long story with interjections from KAREN.

Lights up. LOAN OFFICER is seated at a desk looking over some papers. KAREN enters.

KAREN: Hi. I'm Karen Greendale. I'm here about my car loan.

LOAN OFFICER: Ah yes, Good morning. Please, have a seat. I have your paperwork right here.

KAREN: Great.

LOAN OFFICER: Is this your first car?

KAREN: Yes. My Dad said I had to get one if I wanted an after-school job.

LOAN OFFICER: That's sweet. Will he be co-signing for you?

KAREN: No. He said I had to do this all on my own.

LOAN OFFICER: Very well. I'll have to do a credit history check and a background check to see if you're eligible for a loan.

KAREN: Will that take long?

LOAN OFFICER: Not at all. I can pull it up on the computer right here. It'll only take a few minutes.

KAREN: Great.

LOAN OFFICER: *(Types on computer, looking at paperwork)* Okay, Karen. And is this your correct social security number.

KAREN: Yes, that's me.

LOAN OFFICER: Alright. *(Looks at screen).* Hmm. Oh dear.

KAREN: What is it?

LOAN OFFICER: Well, the computer says you have quite a bit of credit card debt.

KAREN: It does? I wasn't aware that I was carrying a balance. How much?

LOAN OFFICER: Fourteen thousand dollars.

KAREN: Fourteen thousand dollars! How is that possible?

LOAN OFFICER: Do a lot of Christmas shopping?

KAREN: I only have one credit card and I only use it for emergencies.

LOAN OFFICER: Well, that's what the computer says.

KAREN: How did this happen?

LOAN OFFICER: *(Continues looking at screen)* Uh-oh.

KAREN: What?

LOAN OFFICER: Well, it says you also have a home mortgage for over $180,000.

KAREN: A home mortgage?

LOAN OFFICER: Yep $183,316.... and... it looks like it's in default. Having trouble paying your house payment?

KAREN: I live with my parents. I don't own a home.

LOAN OFFICER: I wouldn't live there either if I couldn't afford it.

KAREN: That can't be right.

LOAN OFFICER: This is what the computer says. It also says you have two car loans, a home equity loan, a separate mortgage for a summer home in South Carolina, and an interest-only loan on a large yacht named "Serenity".

KAREN: What?

LOAN OFFICER: Serenity.

KAREN: I don't have any of those things. There's something seriously wrong here.

LOAN OFFICER: It's what the computer says. See I just click here and it pulls up your credit history.

KAREN: That's not my credit history.

LOAN OFFICER: You're Karen Greendale? 749 Lorry Drive?

KAREN: Yes.

LOAN OFFICER: That's you, see? And if I click here I get your background check… Uh-oh.

KAREN: Now what?

LOAN OFFICER: I see you have a few misdemeanors on your record.

KAREN: Misdemeanors?

LOAN OFFICER: On January 8, 2005 you were arrested for driving 137mph in a school zone. Tsk tsk.

KAREN: I wasn't even driving then.

LOAN OFFICER: Then you robbed a liquor store.

KAREN: -That's not me-

LOAN OFFICER: That one's a felony-

KAREN: -There's been some mistake-

LOAN OFFICER: -Took two people hostage-

KAREN: -Someone entered all this stuff wrong-

LOAN OFFICER: -Led the police on a high speed chase ending in a violent collision with a bus full of nuns and orphans.

KAREN: This is ridiculous.

LOAN OFFICER: You served twenty years in a federal prison.

KAREN: I'm sixteen years old!

LOAN OFFICER: *(Sarcastically)* So, how did you enjoy our criminal justice system? Look, Miss Greendale, with this information, we won't be able to grant you your request for a car loan.

KAREN: The information is bogus!

LOAN OFFICER: The computer doesn't lie.

KAREN: It's obviously been input wrong. Your computer is screwed up.

LOAN OFFICER: I can print it out for you if you'd like.

KAREN: I don't need a print out! I need you to correct the information in the file!

LOAN OFFICER: I'll print it just so you have it…. Hmm. It's not working. This computer has been on the fritz all day.

KAREN: AHHHHHHHHHHH!!

Blackout

Signs of Change

David J. Swanson

The Point:

Our beliefs often determine our identity. If we let others restate our beliefs for us, or if we can't articulate why we believe what we believe, we're in danger of losing our identity.

Biblical Reference:

1 Corinthians 16:13, Philippians 1:27, 4, 1 Peter 3:15

Setting:

The student commons at a university.

Cast:

MATT: College kid. Idealistic, but overeager to please.
DJ: Cynic. Not diabolical, but manipulative.
JILL: College girl. Attractive.

Tech needs:

A large whiteboard. A cardboard box. Inside the box, large words are printed on foam board like a giant version of those magnetic word puzzles found on refrigerators. The sketch could also be done with a white board and a marker if the audience is close enough.

Playwright Notes:

This sketch was part of a series we did on keeping your identity. Our Senior Pastor wanted a script that showed how little compromises here and there could end up costing us our witness or our identity as Christians. The sketch uses the interests of an attractive girl as an example of what one could miss out on, but hopefully that is not the take-home point of the sketch.

Be sure that your DJ is not a smarmy unlikable fellow. He's just asking questions and letting MATT hang himself with his own desire to please.

MATT is on stage with a white board. He pulls words out of a box and sticks them to the whiteboard until his sign reads:

I BELIEVE IN GOD

JILL enters.

JILL: Hey, nice sign.

MATT: Thanks. I'm taking a stand. Letting people know who I am.

JILL: I like it. I like when a guy stands up for what he believes. I'm Jill.

MATT: Matt. Nice to meet you.

JILL: I need to get to class, but I hope to see you around. (exits)

DJ enters. Reads sign.

DJ: I like your sign.

MATT: Thanks.

DJ: You're a man of faith, I take it.

MATT: I sure am.

DJ: Hmm. Your sign… Don't you think it's a little narrow minded?

MATT: Narrow minded?

DJ: There are lots of gods out there.

MATT: I only believe in one God.

DJ: Maybe you should specify that.

MATT: Okay. How about this? I believe in A God who is Lord of my life.

He rummages around in box until he brings out a letter "A".

The sign now reads: I BELIEVE IN A GOD

DJ: Lord?

MATT: Yes sir. He has complete control.

DJ: He does?

MATT: That's why I believe in Him. He's in charge of my life.

DJ: He's Lord of your life every single second of every day? You do everything God wants all the time?

MATT: Okay, not exactly every second.

DJ: What about those times when you don't let God be in charge? Do you believe in God then?

MATT: Well yes, but just not as much.

DJ: Then to be perfectly honest, you should say that.

MATT: Fine.

Sign: I MOSTLY BELIEVE IN A GOD

MATT: I've got to be honest, don't I?

DJ: Indeed. Or else God will strike you down.

MATT: Ha. Well, not exactly.

DJ: No lightning bolts?

MATT: No, God's not like that. He lets you live your life. He gives us free choice and all that.

DJ: So he's not up in your face all the time?

MATT: Oh, no.

DJ: Then you need to say that.

Sign: I MOSTLY BELIEVE IN A DISTANT GOD

MATT: Fine. Distant. He gives me my space to live my life and make choices.

DJ: Nice. *(Pause)* But you know…

MATT: What? *(Getting irritated).*

DJ: There are lots of names for God. Some call him Yahweh. Some Allah. Some Jehovah. I mean, isn't that a bit offensive?

MATT: Offensive?

DJ: To presume that you know his name.

MATT: Ugh.

Sign: I MOSTLY BELIEVE IN A DISTANT GOD-LIKE DIETY

MATT: Let's not get caught up on a name. What's important here is that He is glorified.

DJ: He?

MATT: Yes.

DJ: Are you sure your God is a man?

MATT: No, that's just what we say.

DJ: Then shouldn't you-?

MATT: YES! Fine. I'll change the stupid sign.

Sign: I MOSTLY BELIEVE IN A DISTANT GOD-LIKE DIETY OF UNSPECIFIED GENDER.

MATT: Happy?

DJ: Hey, it's not about me. I just wanted to know what you believed. Take care. *(Exits)*

JILL enters.

JILL: Hey, you.

MATT: Hi there.

JILL: I was just thinking about—

(She sees what his sign has become.)

Oh, I'm terribly sorry. I thought you were someone else.

Blackout

Family Feud

David J. Swanson

The Point:

Paul was a unique thinker. After his conversion, Paul went from persecuting Christians to being the most effective missionary in the history of Christianity. His thinking was 180 degrees from the conventional wisdom of the time.

Biblical Reference:

1 Peter 2:11, Romans 12, 13, Galatians 1:11-16

Setting:

The final round of the game show "Family Feud".

Cast:

HOST:	Cheesy game show host.
THADDEUS:	Pharisee
PAUL:	Radical apostle.

Tech needs:

The big challenge to this sketch is the game board projected onto a video screen. We did this with a PowerPoint slideshow that stepped through the answers and clock as needed. Also, getting the proper sound effects adds quite a bit to the believability of the game show.

Playwright Notes:

This is a fun sketch sure to make your audience laugh. The underlying theme here is to highlight the difference in thinking between Paul and the Pharisees. A good presentation of game board and sound effects, along with some over-the-top performances will really bring this sketch home.

Game show rejoinder music.

Lights up.

SLIDE: Family Feud Title Slide

HOST and THADDEUS stand together in front of the Family Feud board.

Audience applause.

HOST: Hi and welcome back to The Family Feud. Our winning team this week is the Pharisee family and they get to play the final Fast Money round. Now THADDEUS, your team has elected that you go first. Who else did your team select?

THADDEUS: Saul.

HOST: Ah, you mean PAUL. He goes by PAUL now.

THADDEUS: Yes. Him.

HOST: Are you sure? During the game today there seemed to quite a bit of disagreement between PAUL and the rest of the family.

THADDEUS: We're confident that Saul is a little less radical now and ready to play the feud.

HOST: Alright, let's do that. PAUL is backstage in our isolation booth and cannot hear your answers. THADDEUS you will have 20 seconds to answer five questions from our survey. Try to name the most popular answers from a survey of 100 Jews. Are you ready?

THADDEUS: I'm ready.

HOST: Can we have 20 seconds on the clock? And begin.

Slide: Clock to 20 Seconds. Begins countdown.

(Clock tick sound effect)

HOST: A man steals from the temple but later confesses. What do you do with him?

THADDEUS: Stone him!

HOST: What do you do with a woman is accused of being a prostitute?

THADDEUS: Stone her!

HOST: What do you do with a man who claims to be the Messiah?

THADDEUS: Stone him!

HOST: What would you do if someone attacked you for preaching.

THADDEUS: Run away. Get some friends. Then stone him!

HOST: What do you do when a Gentile enters the temple.

THADDEUS: Stone him!

HOST: Okay, very good. Let's see how you did, THADDEUS.

(They turn to face the board)

You'll get a point for every person that answered the same way. If, after PAUL's round, the two of you have 200 points, you'll win the grand prize of 1000 Denarii! Let's see how you did. A man steals from the temple but later confesses. What do you do with him? You said,

Slide: Stone him

"Stone Him". Survey said,

Slide: 47

Forty-seven! Wow. Off to a great start. What do you do with a woman is accused of being a prostitute? You said, "Stone her".

Slide: Stone her

Survey said,

Slide: 38

Thirty-eight, very good. Third question: What do you do with a man who claims to be the Messiah? You said "Stone him".

Slide: Stone him

> Survey said,

Slide: 41

> Very good, THADDEUS.   What would you do if someone attacked you for preaching? You said "Run then Stone."

Slide: Run Then Stone

> Survey said,

Slide: 33

> And finally, What do you do when a Gentile enters the temple. You enthusiastically said "Stone him."

Slide: Stone him

> And the survey said,

Slide: 40

> Forty!. For a total of 199. Excellent THADDEUS. PAUL needs only one more point and your family wins the grand prize! Let's cover the answers and bring out PAUL now.

THADDEUS: Let's go Saul. You can do it!

HOST: Okay, Paul. I can't tell you how many points you have, but I'll tell you that Thaddeus did remarkably well.

PAUL: Great!

HOST: Your team is in great shape. I'll read you five questions which you must answer. If you repeat an answer THADDEUS gave, I'll ask you to try again. Answer these five questions and you'll get out of here with 1000 Denarii!

PAUL: Get out of here? Where am I going? I'm under house arrest.

HOST: 20 seconds on the clock please. And begin.

(clock tick sound effect)

	A man steals from the temple but later confesses. What do you do with him?
PAUL:	Forgive him.
HOST:	What do you do with a woman is accused of being a prostitute?
PAUL:	Don't cast the first stone.
HOST:	What do you do with a man who claims to be the Messiah?
PAUL:	If he's the Messiah, follow him.
HOST:	What would you do if someone attacked you for preaching?
PAUL:	Keep preaching!
HOST:	What do you do when a Gentile enters the Temple?
PAUL:	Embrace him as a brother and share the gospel!
HOST:	Okay. That's good. Well, you certainly didn't repeat any answers. Let's look at the board.
PAUL:	Whoa! 199 points!
HOST:	That's right. The first question: A man steals from the temple but later confesses. What do you do with him? You said. "Forgive him".

Slide: Forgive Him

Survey said.

Slide: 0

Ooh. Stone him. Number one answer.

THADDEUS:	Forgive him? Are you kidding, Saul?
PAUL:	Sorry THADDEUS, that's what I'd do.
HOST:	No worries, there are four more questions to get that one point you need. What do you do with a woman who is accused of being a prostitute? You said "No stoning".

Slide: No Stoning

Survey said

Slide: 0

Zero. Too bad.

THADDEUS: Saul, we went over this in synagogue!

HOST: What do you do with a man who claims to be the Messiah? You said "Follow him".

Slide: Follow him

Survey said

Slide: 0

THADDEUS: Follow him! Are you an idiot! He's a blasphemer!

PAUL: Not if he's the Messiah.

HOST: Settle down you two, there're two questions left. What would you do if someone attacked you for preaching? You said "Keep preaching".

Slide: Keep Preaching

Survey said

Slide: 0

Zero. Run away, number one answer.

THADDEUS: Just answer the stinkin' questions, Saul!

PAUL: My name is PAUL. And I answered it correctly.

HOST: Okay, one last chance. Remember, you just need one, measly, little point. What do you do when a gentile enters the temple? You said "Hug him".

Slide: Hug him

For 1000 Denarii, survey said

Slide: 0

ZERO!

THADDEUS: I'm gonna kill you Saul!

HOST: Oh, I'm so sorry, your team wins nothing.

THADDEUS: *(Begins comically choking PAUL)*

You little…

PAUL: Help! I'm being persecuted! Help!

HOST: Join us next week for Family Feud where we pit the Nero family

versus the German Barbarians. Thanks and good night!

PAUL: Ahhhh! Run!

THADDEUS: Get back here!

Cue game show outro music.

THADDEAU chases PAUL him out of auditorium.

Blackout

Christian Living

The Practical Side

Dead or Alive

David J. Swanson

The Point:

1. Are you alive in Christ? Does anyone know?
2. The belief that Christ didn't die on the cross and that the Roman soldiers mistook him for dead is as ridiculous as a modern day CSI crew mistaking a living person for dead.

Biblical Reference:

Revelation 3:16, Matthew 27:32-62, Luke 24:46, Galatians 2:20, Romans 6:3-8

Setting:

A Saturday afternoon in the park. LAURA is lying under a tree reading a book and enjoying her lunch.

Cast:

LAURA:	Normal teenage girl. Not dead.
HOLLY:	Normal teenage girl. Friend of LAURA.
GIL:	CSI Lead Investigator
CATHERINE:	CSI Investigator
COP:	Cop at the scene.
SAM SPADE:	1930's era detective. Chauvinist. Tough guy.

Tech needs:

CSI video, birds chirping sound effect, film noir saxophone music, trench coat, fedora, sandwich, evidence bag, latex gloves.

Playwright Notes:

This sketch was originally written to illustrate how ludicrous it would be for a trained Roman soldier to mistake Jesus for dead if he was really alive. However, there's a larger point here that could be used in other contexts. This could be used as a metaphor for people who are alive in Christ but no one knows it.

For this sketch we went to the extraordinary lengths of making a mock "CSI: Wichita" video to play at the beginning of a series of sketches. This was the first in the series.

SFX: *Birds chirping, then tension filled music as HOLLY enters.*

HOLLY enters from stage right. Approaches LAURA on ground.

HOLLY: Laura? Laura? Are you here? Your mom said that you were here at the park? Laura? *Sees LAURA.*

LAURA: Hey, Holly.

HOLLY: Screams. *(Blood curdling scream)*

Blackout

CSI type opening video to set up a cop-drama television show.

Lights up. Same scene but with police tape around it. GIL and CATHERINE, two CSI agents, enter and approach COP, already on the scene. HOLLY is bundled up in a blanket sitting USR.

GIL: *(Shows badge to COP).* CSI. So what've you got?

COP: Dead white, teenage girl. 17 years old. No signs of struggle. No blood.

LAURA: Um, hello?

All ignore LAURA.

CATHERINE: Who found her?

COP:	Her friend, over there. Also 17. Her name's Holly. She says she was best friends with the victim. Says she was meeting the vic for lunch here in the park. You can talk with her if you want.
GIL:	Did you get the victim's name?
COP:	Laura Mitchell from Goddard.
LAURA:	*(Sits up.)* Hey, that's me!
CATHERINE:	How'd she die?
COP:	*(Shrugs).* Undetermined. That's why we called you. Oh, one more thing. District is sending in a specialist.
CATHERINE:	A specialist?
COP:	Yeah, a real hot-shot detective. Don't let him get in your way. *(Exits.)*
GIL:	Great. Just what we needed: more interference from District.
LAURA:	Uh, excuse me? Can I help you guys?
CATHERINE:	*(Moves towards HOLLY).* Holly, do you mind if we ask you some questions?
HOLLY:	I already gave my testimony to the police.
GIL:	I know, but we'd like to ask you a few more questions. We're crime scene investigators. Did Laura come to the park often?
HOLLY:	She'd often bring her lunch and sit and read here in the park... I just can't believe she's dead.
LAURA:	I'm not dead.
CATHERINE:	*(Searching around body.)* Hey I found something. (Holds up half eaten sandwich. Puts it in plastic bag.)
LAURA:	Hey! That's my lunch.
HOLLY:	She always loved Peanut Butter and Jelly... *(Sobs)*

SFX: 1930's style detective music. Detective SAM SPADE enters wearing long trench coat with collar turned up, hat and an intense look about him.

SAM: Sorry I'm late, schweethaht. What seems to be the trouble?

GIL: Are you the detective District sent?

SAM: Name's Sam Spade, Private Investigator. I solve crimes. It's what I
            do.

CATHERINE: Well, we've got our own investigation underway. So if you don't
            mind, you can stay out of our way until we're done here.

SAM steps forward to talk directly to audience in monologue.

SAM: I could tell that this dame was going to be a tough nut to crack. I
            had a job to do. And no two-bit crime scene investigator was
            going to get in my way.
            (Returns to scene.)
            Oh, I'll stay out of your way, but first, give me the low-down on the
            dead broad.

CATHERINE: *(Rolls eyes).* Fine. Laura Mitchell. 17. Found dead in this park two
            hours ago.

SAM: Find anything out of the ordinary?

CATHERINE: Just this sandwich.

SAM: Great, I'm starving. *(Takes sandwich and starts eating.)*

GIL: Hey that's evidence!

SAM: Well I can't solve this crime on an empty stomach. Hey, how
            'bout getting me a drink, Dollface? Scotch on the rocks.

CATHERINE: *(Insulted).* I'm in the middle of an investigation.

SAM: *(Condescending)* Sure you are, sweetheart. Sure you are. Who
            found the girl?

LAURA: Excuse me, I'm not dead. I'm just resting. *(Gets up walks cross
            stage behind everyone.)* See? I'm moving. Not dead.

GIL: Her friend Holly found the body here. *(Turns to look at where
            LAURA was lying.)* Great, someone has moved the body.

SAM:	You lost the body?
GIL:	Catherine. Did you authorize them to move the body?
CATHERINE:	No.
SAM:	Ah. The great mystery of the disappearing corpse.
LAURA:	I'm not a corpse!
SAM:	Are you sure the dame was dead?
GIL:	We're trained professionals. We'd know if she wasn't dead.
SAM:	(*Aside to audience*). I was starting to wonder if these clowns would know if their own noses were still attached to their face. It was time to do something. Something drastic.
	(*Suddenly grabs GIL by the collar*).
	All right, you no good punk! I'm on to your little scam. Now you're going to tell me everything.
GIL:	What the--?
CATHERINE:	Stop that. Let him go. You're hurting him.
SAM:	You stay out of this, Sugarlips! (*To GIL*). What have you done? What's the game?
GIL:	I don't know what you're talking about.
SAM:	Don't you? Well maybe this will help explain things!

SAM pulls out revolver. LAURA screams. Everyone hears her and reacts.

HOLLY:	Laura!
GIL:	Holy cow. She's alive!
CATHERINE:	It's a miracle!
SAM:	Is it? It's not a miracle if she was never dead. (Crosses to LAURA. Softly.) Are you okay, honey?
LAURA:	(*Annoyed*). Yes. That's what I've been trying to tell you.
HOLLY:	(*Hugs Laura*). Don't ever do that to me again.
LAURA:	Can I go home now?

SAM: Sure, Dollface. Just tell me one thing. *(Dramatically.)* Why did you do it?

LAURA: *(Pause).* You people are crazy.

LAURA and HOLLY exit.

SAM: *(Aside to audience).* Of course, it was all starting to make sense now. The sandwich. The park. The CSI crew that couldn't tell the difference between a herd of elephants and a coffee table.

GIL: So I guess since there was no crime, we don't need to be here. I still don't get how we missed it. All that evidence and she wasn't even dead.

SAM: There're some mysteries in life, that you just can't solve.

CATHERINE: Let's get out of here. Sam, you coming?

SAM: Sure thing. You know, I think this is the beginning of a beautiful friendship.

They exit together. Music swells.

Blackout

Christian Robot Replacement

David J. Swanson

The Point:

Going through the motions of the Christian life is a pointless exercise that robs you of your communion with God and your fellowship with others.

Biblical Reference:

I John 1: 3-7

Setting:

An infomercial on TV for a new product. Modern day. Marla starts stage center. ROBOT is Stage Right and covered by a sheet.

Cast:

STAGE MANAGER:	Sets tone of infomercial. Introduces cue cards.
MARLA MOPPINS:	Peppy host who poorly acts surprised, awed and wowed by the features of the product.
SKIP TUMALOO:	Over-excited salesman who introduces and describes the product for sale.
ROBOT:	Robot performs stands stiffly and artificially, but delivers his lines naturally and fluidly before resetting to a stiff and artificially pose.

Tech Needs:

Cue cards, headset for stage manager, intro music, sheet to cover robot.

Playwright Notes:

Sadly, there are people in the church who are no less robotic in their Christian walk than this "robot". Do what you can to make this feel like an infomercial. Cheesy presentation, stock production music, audience participation will bring the scene about.

When bringing on the actor playing the robot, put a sheet over him and have someone else carry him on stage. It'll help the audience with their suspension of disbelief needed for this sketch to work.

Lights up. STAGE MANAGER enters with stack of cue cards.

STAGE MANAGER:

Hello audience. Thank you so much for volunteering to be in our infomercial. Now we promise to put lots of shots of the audience in the program, but we need to see lots of interested, excited people to help us sell the product. So, to help you out, I'll be giving you these cues at the appropriate time. Let's go ahead and practice this one time so we're ready for the show.

(Goes through signs, audience gives appropriate response.)

Okay. It looks like we're ready. Roll music!

Cheesy Production Music Intro.

(CUE CARD: Applause)

MARLA: Hello and welcome to "Simply Amazing"; the only show on TV that brings you something amazing every time. I'm Marla Moppins and today we have something truly amazing that will change the way you go about your everyday Christian life. My guest today is accomplished inventor-Skip Tumaloo!

(CUE CARD: Applause)

SKIP runs out on stage excited and full of energy to the applause of the crowd.

SKIP: Well, hello and thank you, Marla. I am so excited about what I'm about to show you.

MARLA: I can hardly wait, Skip.

SKIP: Let me ask you something. What's the hardest part about going to church?

MARLA: You mean besides tithing? *(Forced laughter)*

(CUE CARD: Laugh.)

I guess it would have to be interacting with all the other Christians.

SKIP: "Interacting with other Christians." What do you mean by that?

MARLA: Well, I mean people ask me how I'm doing and I have to put on my "Christian smile" and say the right things. I mean, faking all that sincerity can be quite draining.

SKIP: So why don't you quit going to church?

MARLA: Are you kidding? Most of my friends go to church. It's expected that I go. Not to mention the free breakfast at Sunday School, the beautiful music, and the fun social opportunities during the week. *(Downhearted)* No, I guess I'm stuck spending my Sunday mornings at church, right?

SKIP: Wrong!

(Crossing to ROBOT)

Marla, let me introduce you to the latest in Christian Robot Replacement.

(Unveils ROBOT)

Meet the T4000.

(CUE CARD: OOH-AHH)

MARLA: Wow, Skip! Did you say Christian Robot Replacement?

SKIP: That's right Marla! The T4000 can be custom ordered to match your appearance exactly. Once programmed with your mannerisms, quirks and other... abnormalities, this Christian Robot Replacement can take your place at any religious function.

MARLA: Now, that's amazing!

(CUE CARD: Applause).

But, come on, Skip. No one is going to be fooled by a robot with a preprogrammed personality.

SKIP: Give her a try. Let me just set him to "Sunday Morning"

(Pulls out remote. Points at ROBOT and pushes a button.)

OK, go ahead....

MARLA: Uh... Did you enjoy the service this morning?

ROBOT: Oh, yes, very much. It's like a spiritual recharge every week. The Pastor had quite a few points I hadn't thought about before. And the music was so uplifting.

MARLA: Wow, just like a real Christian!

SKIP: Exactly.

MARLA: Holy cow, Skip. This truly is amazing! So, what you're saying is that I could send a Christian Robot Replacement to church Sunday morning while I'm home reading the paper or sleeping in?

SKIP: Why not? That's where your mind is anyway. You see Marla; your life is too short to waste time going through the motions at church. The T4000 keeps you wonderfully insulated from any accountability, sin confrontation, or theological discussion of any kind.

MARLA: That's amazing!

(CUE CARD: Applause)

Now Skip, I've seen some low quality robots, and they really don't do the job when you start looking at the details. Does this Christian Robot Replacement have what it takes?

SKIP: In spades. The T4000 has a number of features new to robotic replacements. For instance it has "Generalized Struggling".

MARLA: "Generalized Struggling?" What's that?

SKIP: Why don't we find out? Ask her if you can pray for her.

MARLA: Uh, OK. (To ROBOT) Is there anything I can be praying for in your life, Ms. uh Robot.

ROBOT: Yeah, I'm struggling with a few things right now. I have some sin in my life, and I would appreciate your prayers about that.

SKIP: You see, it seems like the robot is being sincere, but it's doing it without allowing anyone to get close enough to find out that it's actually a robot.

MARLA: And would that be bad? Someone getting close to it?

SKIP: Disastrous. The T4000 is not designed for heart to heart, one-on-one sharing and bonding. Relationship building is the last thing you want to do with a Christian Robot Replacement.

MARLA: Well, what if my robot is asked into…say, a circle of prayer? Will it be up to the challenge?

SKIP: He sure is, Marla. The T4000 comes equipped a feature I call the "Amen Squeeze".

MARLA: The "Amen Squeeze"?

SKIP: Yeah. Pretend to form a circle and finish a prayer with it.

MARLA: All right.

     (Takes ROBOT's hand. ROBOT bows head as SKIP points remote at him.)

     …we pray these things in Jesus' name. Amen. OH! It squeezed my hand! Just like a real Christian! It's like it sincerely cares about me.

SKIP: But she doesn't! She's a robot, remember?

MARLA: Oh yeah. I keep having to remind myself.

They laugh.

SKIP: Now, I know what you're wondering. The T4000 is the right Christian Robot Replacement for me. But how much? Right?

MARLA:	You read my mind, Skip. What will this cost me?
SKIP:	Well, before I give you the price, let me just tell you that you not only get the T4000, but you also get this pre-highlighted Bible. This Bible has over 98% of the verses highlighted to fool any doubter.

(CUE CARD: Ohh-Ahh)

MARLA:	But, at what price, Skip?
SKIP:	Not so fast Marla. Try picking up the Robot.
MARLA:	Picking it up?
SKIP:	Yeah, give it a lift.

MARLA lifts ROBOT easily from the waist then puts him down.

MARLA:	Wow. It's so lightweight! How is it that it weighs so little?
SKIP:	That's the biggest secret of all. Thanks to the latest in fiber optics and piezoelectric motivation the T4000 is completely hollow inside.

They both stare strangely into the blackness for a few seconds.

MARLA:	*(Starting to realize the truth.)*
	It's… completely…. hollow?
SKIP:	Completely. There's no substance of any kind inside.
MARLA:	Nothing inside? Nothing at all?… not… not even a heart?
SKIP:	Nothing but utter darkness.
MARLA:	Oh… I… I see.
SKIP:	That's the beauty of it. And no one has to know because he looks so good from the outside.
MARLA:	*(Slowly)* But if I send a Christian Robot Replacement to church for me… what happens to my relationships? My friendships with other Christians?
SKIP:	*(Uncomfortable but faking a smile. Under his breath)* Uh, Marla. That's not in the script…
MARLA:	What happens with my walk with God?

SKIP: *(Laughs nervously).* These aren't the things you should be worried about.

MARLA: And all I'll be left with is....

(She looks at ROBOT).

I'm sorry Skip.

(Gathers things to leave.)

I need to leave. I have some praying to do.

SKIP: Why don't you let the T4000 do it for you? Wait! Where are you going? I haven't even told you how much this is going to cost you yet!

MARLA: No, Skip. You showed me. *(Exits)*

Blackout

No Complaints

David J. Swanson

The Point:

Complaining is often disrespectful and hurtful, and shows immaturity.

Biblical Reference:

Philippians 4:2

Setting:

Five high school friends are hanging out on a Friday night at KATIE's parents' house with a movie and some food.

Cast:

KURT-   Constantly complaining teenager
JEREMY-   KURT's like minded best friend.
KATIE-   Feisty teenage hostess for party
BETH-   Caring teenage friend.
JESSICA-   Amiable, mild mannered, long suffering, teenager.

Tech Needs:

Couch, bags of food, plate of cookies, DVD case, table.

Playwright Notes:

It can be a habit, amongst both teenagers and adults, to complain all the time without even realizing it. Some hide behind "well, I'm just telling the truth," but it doesn't excuse a complaining heart. Allow this sketch to run its dramatic course. Don't rush it. The interplay between characters needs time to develop. All five actors should be really close friends and their familiarity should be obvious.

This sketch hinges on the audiences empathy for JESSICA.

Lights fade in.

KURT, JEREMY, and KATIE are in the middle of a conversation in KATIE's basement.

KURT: So I'm like, "Dad, hello?" There's no way this clunker is going to get me to and from school every day.

JEREMY: *(To KATIE)*

You should see it, KATIE. It is a total pile. I think it's got more rust than paint.

KATIE: (They laugh)

That's so funny. You in a 1998 Cavalier.

KURT: I know…. I think my Dad hates me.

KATIE: *(Laughs)* Well at least you've got a car, Kurt. My parents keep telling me that riding the school bus builds character.

JEREMY: Yeah, why is it that everything that seems to build character also saves Mom and Dad money?

BETH enters with local grocery store bags of food.

BETH: Hey guys. I got dinner.

JEREMY: Sweet. I'm starving.

BETH: I've got chicken, chips, potato salad and soda.

KURT: *(Sarcastically)* Nothing like a home cooked meal. You'll make a great wife someday Beth.

BETH: *(Laughing)* Oh shut up, you. Just be glad my parents bought dinner for us.

JEREMY: So who else is coming?

KATIE: I think just Jessica. Everyone else I called was busy. *(To the boys)* Why don't you two go pick out a DVD for us to watch? My Dad keeps them next to the TV upstairs.

KURT: Seriously? You want us to pick the movie?

KATIE: Yeah. You always say you hate the movies we pick anyway.

KURT: Fine by me. Let's go. *(They exit)*

BETH: *(Shouting after them)*
And not *Dodgeball!*

KURT and JEREMY: *(Offstage)* Awww.

BETH: Why'd you let them pick the movie?

KATIE: I just get tired of hearing them whine whenever we pick a movie that takes more than two brain cells to understand.

BETH: *(Smiling)* No kidding....

JESSICA enters with plate of cookies.

JESSICA: Hey guys!

BETH: Jess! You made it. (Seeing the cookies) Ooh, and you brought dessert!

JESSICA: *(Setting cookies down on coffee table)* I thought I'd try my Mom's old recipe. They're raisin nut cookies.

KATIE: Wow. You cooked? I didn't know you liked to bake.

JESSICA: I just got into it. It's something my Mom and I can do together.

BETH: Cool.

JESSICA: Where're Kurt and Jeremy?

KATIE: Oh they just went to pick out the movie. They should be down soon. We can go ahead and start eating, though.

They start to dish up plates of food for themselves. KURT and JEREMY enter with DVD case.

KURT: Katie, your Dad's DVD collection sucks.

JEREMY:	Yeah, like half of his movies are black and white. I think they're from the Civil War or something like that.
KATIE:	*(A little annoyed)* I'm sorry that's all we have. Didn't you find anything to watch?
KURT:	Yeah, we found- (sees plate of cookies) Ooh! Cookies! You didn't tell us you bought cookies. *(Rushes over to grab and eat cookie)*
JEREMY:	Yeah, I love (grocery store) cookies! *(Following him, eats as well)*
KATIE:	Actually…
KURT:	Oh, gross! (Spits out cookie) I hope you got a receipt!
JEREMY:	*(Spitting his out too)* What do these have bugs in them?! *(Hacking)*
BETH:	You guys, stop! *(Embarrassed for JESSICA)* They're raisin nut cookies.
KURT:	I don't care what they are. They're terrible! *(Continuing to spit out cookie and wipe his mouth)*
JEREMY:	Why didn't you just get chocolate chip? Yuck…These taste like dog poop. (They start to laugh)
KATIE:	*(Yelling. Angry.)* You guys, stop it!

Silence. KURT and JEREMY are taken aback by KATIE's yelling and have a "What's your problem" look on their faces. KATIE and BETH turn to JESSICA. She is devastated.

JESSICA:	*(Trying to control her feelings).* Katie. Don't- just….don't. (She takes the plate of cookies and exits)
BETH:	*(Upset)* You are such a jerk!
KURT:	What? Why?
KATIE:	JESSICA made those for us! We didn't buy them.

JEREMY: What? (Defensively, somewhat apologetically) Well, we didn't know…

KURT: Why didn't you tell us? We didn't mean to hurt her feelings.

JEREMY: I would have never said that if I had known she made them.

KATIE: You shouldn't say that stuff anyway.

JEREMY: Why? (Getting more defensive. Cautiously) Look, I know it was harsh and all, but we were just telling the truth.

KURT: Yeah. I'm sorry she's so sensitive and all, but we were just expressing our opinions.

BETH: I don't believe you two!

KATIE: (Angry) All right, look. They were free! If you didn't like them, then don't eat them. It's that simple. Keep your comments to yourself.

BETH: Try being a little more grateful, okay?

JESSICA enters with empty plate.

JESSICA: (Trying to smile it off, still hurt.) Well, we won't have those around to ruin our evening.

KATIE: Aw, Jess… You threw them away?

JESSICA: Yeah. I'll get Mom to try a different recipe next time.

KURT: Jess…. I didn't mean to hurt your feelings. I thought Beth got them at the grocery store.

JESSICA: (Still trying to downplay her hurt)

Eh, don't worry about it. They're just cookies, right?

(Breath) So how about that movie…

JEREMY: Uh, yeah. I got it right here….

General somber milling about as they get food. The episode has dampened their mood and made everything awkward. Awkward small talk. Everything is not all right.

Slow fade to black.

Love Language

David J. Swanson

The Point:

Not everyone gives or receives love and appreciation the same way.

Biblical Reference:

Ecclesiastes 10:12, Proverbs 18:21, 2 Corinthians 9:7, Luke 6:38, Matthew 26: 6-13

Setting:

An office.

Cast:

TED- Man, mid 30s-50s. Office employee who expresses appreciation through gift giving.

JACK- Man, mid 30s-50s. Office employee who expresses appreciation through service.

Tech needs:

Chair, desk, office stuff on desk, presents, stapler, daily calendars.

Playwright Notes:

Love means more than romantic love. This sketch echoes "The Odd Couple" with two platonic co-workers dealing with each other's personality. Let the first five lines or so be played with a boring machismo before the contorted and slightly awkward working relationship is revealed.

Two co-workers return to the job after the Christmas holiday. On stage are a

chair and a desk. On the desk are a computer, a stapler, a mug with pens in it and an empty daily calendar. JACK enters, takes off his coat and sits down, placing a new daily calendar on the desk. After a few seconds of getting settled, a knock is heard and TED enters.

TED: Morning, Jack.

JACK: Good Morning, Ted.

TED: How was your Christmas?

JACK: Fine. Now it's back the old grind, huh? How was your vacation?

TED: The best. Carol and I had a great time in Colorado. In fact....

Guess what?

(Rummages through briefcase to find present)

JACK: You got me something.

TED: *(Not hearing him)*

We got you something!

JACK: I should have guessed. Ted, you really shouldn't-

TED: Oh, just open it. It's a belated Christmas gift.

JACK: *(Opens gift)*

A pair of winter gloves. Well, that's very nice of you. Thank you.

(TED stands expectantly)

JACK: Oh! Oh, sorry. Of course, I've got something for you.

(TED lights up).

Uh... I didn't have time to wrap it...

(Looks over desk)

Here you are.

(Hands TED a stapler)

TED: A stapler?

JACK: Yeah, I thought you could use it to, uh, staple things.

TED: *(Pause)* Jack, we need to talk.

JACK:	Oh?
TED:	I know it's not a big deal, and I try to ignore it, but this is really getting to me.
JACK:	What do you mean?
TED:	Remember when I got you that golf shirt for Thanksgiving? What did you get me?
JACK:	Uh...
TED:	A three-hole punch. And for Halloween, I got you some movie tickets. What did you get me?
JACK:	I honestly don't remember.
TED:	Half a stack of post-it notes. And the top page had a phone number written on it that you needed.
JACK:	Right.
TED:	At Labor Day, I got you a Shockers ball cap and you got me a mechanical pencil, three paper clips and a button. Do you see where I'm going with this?
JACK:	I know that I haven't put a lot of thought into your gifts-
TED:	You haven't put ANY thought into my gifts! You're just grabbing stuff off of your desk and handing it to me! It's all stuff I can get in the supply closet anyway. At first I thought that I had just surprised you, caught you off guard. But come on, Jack. *(TED is obviously hurt).*
JACK:	You do catch me off guard! Who gives gifts to each other on Labor Day? Seriously! How am I supposed to know that you're getting me something for Halloween? It's just too much!
TED:	*(Sarcastic, biting)* Well I'm sorry! Where I grew up you gave gifts to people you cared about. You gave an apple to the teacher, a gift certificate to the

mailman and gifts to your coworkers on holidays. That's how I was brought up! What's worse is you don't even appreciate it.

JACK: I do appreciate it, Ted.

TED: Do you like working with me or not?

JACK: I do. You're a great guy to work with....

TED: Well then why don't you show some appreciation every once in a while?

JACK: Ted, you're starting to sound like my wife.

TED: *(Insulted, hysterical)*

What's that supposed to mean?

JACK: Sorry, I didn't mean that. But while we're on the subject of appreciation, how about that time I helped you with the Marshall account?

TED: What of it?

JACK: You had to have that presentation done and you were going to be here all night. Remember?

TED: *(Pause, thinking)*

...Which account?

JACK: The Marshall account! We were both here until 11 o'clock at night. You don't remember that?

TED: Kinda.

JACK: Kinda? That's what I mean Ted. You didn't say one thank-you, not one note of appreciation. I missed dinner with the kids that night to help you out....

TED: I got you a Thanksgiving Day present.

JACK: That was two weeks later! A few words of thanks would have meant a lot more! *(Now JACK is furious)*

They sit, letting the angry words hover around them

TED: (*Quietly*) I'm sorry.

(*Pause*)

Do you want a hug?

JACK: No! You know what? Forget it. Just forget it. I'm going for some coffee.

(*JACK takes jacket and leaves*)

TED: Wait. Don't you want to see what I got you for New Year's?

TED follows JACK off stage, another present in hand.

Blackout

Catwalk of Shame

David J. Swanson

The Point:

Mimicking God means looking and acting like Him. Anything self-serving or anything unlike God is filthy rags. It's not funny, it's not fun, and it will destroy what we care about most.

Biblical Reference:

Ephesians 5:1-7

Setting:

The runway for a fashion show. Thumping dance music. Lights flashing. A polished announcer and fashion designer, stand stage right with handheld mics.

Cast:

CAMERON: Professional MC. Polished announcer.
DEVO: Eccentric fashion designer. Pretentious and outlandish. Diva. Speaks with thick German or Russian accent.
MODEL 1: Female model.
MODEL 2: Female model.
MODEL 3: Male model. Ugly American

Tech needs:

This was one of our most difficult sketches from a tech point of view. It requires dance club-like lights to set the mood, a techno track, and some elaborate costumes. The effect, however was substantial and was a welcome diversion from simpler black-box theater sketches.

Playwright Notes:

The difficulties in costuming, lighting and sound are well worth the effort with this poignant but light-hearted sketch. The key to this sketch is to realize that the model at the end should be ugly. If he's hilarious, the sketch loses its way. Saying you're dressed in God clothes while dressed in filthy rags is repulsive and the end of the sketch should reflect this.

Blackout

Techno music begins at full volume. Flashing, club-like lights up 6-10 seconds later, bring up stage lights. MODEL 2 is showing off her contemporary dress. CAMERON stands off to the side holding a handheld mic.

MODEL 2 exits stage wearing normal clothing just finishing the last of a normal fashion collection.

Music fades out.

CAMERON: Thank you, ladies. And that concludes the Winter 2011 collection, Giuseppe, from famed Italian designer Giuseppe Luigi. How about a round of applause for Giuseppe. Well, ladies and gentlemen, it's time for the moment we've all been waiting for. Our last collection is from an industry icon who has single handedly transformed the fashion industry. Please welcome the man known simply as Devo.

DEVO enters.

DEVO: Thank you, Miss Cameron. Enough with this frivolity. Let us get to the collection.

CAMERON: Well, I'm not the only one eager to see what genius you've created for us this year. Tell us a little about the collection.

Music restarts, quietly, under dialogue.

DEVO: Cam, this has to be one of my best collections of all time. The collection will be known as *(dramatic pause)* Le Bible.

CAMERON: Le Bible? Tell us about it.

DEVO: Le Bible draws inspiration from some of the oldest spiritual texts known to man. Le Bible is the result of many minutes one night searching the pages of a Holy Bible that was left in my hotel room. Its timelessness will only be surpassed by its grounded doctrine.

MODEL 1 enters. She wears a Coat of Many Colors made into a slightly different style.

CAMERON: Here's our first piece. Now this is a colorful coat that can be worn in all seasons.

DEVO: Yes, this Technicolor dream coat derives its inspiration from Joseph and his coat of many colors. It says love, it says uniqueness, it says pizzazz.

CAMERON: Oh, Devo, it's wonderful.

DEVO: It's also being sold with a sensible clutch.

As MODEL 1 finishes, MODEL 2 enters wearing breastplate, helmet, belt and normal clothes underneath.

CAMERON: Your second piece is for those looking for a more armored look.

DEVO: For those looking to put on the full armor of God, we have this breastplate of righteousness with a svelte belt of truth. You can wear this with or without the helmet of salvation, though I highly recommend going with the helmet.

CAMERON: It's such a versatile look, Devo. You can wear it to parties, to concerts where there might be some moshing and you need some protection.

DEVO: And it's a smash at Renaissance festivals.

CAMERON: Good point.

DEVO: It says strength, it says moxie-

CAMERON: It says expect delays while going through airport security. *(Laughs at her own joke. DEVO is annoyed.)* Sorry. Tell us about our next piece.

MODEL 2 exits. MODEL 1 enters wearing torn veil.

DEVO: Cam, this piece attempts to capture that critical moment in time when Christ died upon the cross and the veil in the temple was torn in two. It's difficult to get one's mind around. Its high-concept. Very abstract.

CAMERON: No, actually it's quite literal. You have a veil and you tore it in two.

DEVO: Yes, but the WAY I tore it in two is the genius behind it.

CAMERON: How's that?

DEVO: Like this

(Mimes tearing some fabric in two).

CAMERON: *(Sarcastically)* Brilliant.

DEVO: I thought you'd think so.

CAMERON: Our last piece I've been told is the piece de resistance.

DEVO: This last piece is my masterpiece, Cam. I call it Godclothes.

CAMERON: God clothes?

DEVO: Yes, it attempts to reflect the pureness of God. The simple brilliance in being all that is good and nothing that is not. Holiness, Cam. Holiness is what God is all about.

CAMERON: Where is the model? *(to stagehand)* Steve, is there a problem?

MODEL 3 staggers on stage. He wears a filthy shirt and torn pants. He staggers around in stark contrast to the other model's walk. He wears an expression of selfishness and mockery.

MODEL 3:   Sorry I'm late. *(To audience member)* Hey, you're pretty. Ugh, the flashing lights are not good for my hangover. Can we turn them off, for cryin' out loud?

Music stops. Lights go steady.

CAMERON: Oh Cam, it's brilliant. How very existential!

MODEL 3 falls down.

MODEL 3:   Oh I can't see straight.

DEVO: *(Furious)*

What is this outrage!?!

MODEL 3:   *(Gets back up.)*

I'm on a catwalk. Look at me!

DEVO: Who? What is this?

MODEL 3:   *(Sings)* Oh, don't you wish your girlfriend was hot like me? Haha. Yeah, people!

DEVO: You imbecile! You've ruined my show.

DEVO attacks MODEL 3 and chases him backstage.

CAMERON: Oh my. I guess this concludes our show. I'd like to thank Devo.

DEVO: *(Offstage)* IDIOT!

CAMERON: See you next time. *(Exits)*

Blackout

Discipleship

David J. Swanson

The Point:

Getting saved isn't the end of the Christian walk, it's the beginning. And a healthy Christian needs discipleship to grow.

Biblical Reference:

Matthew 28:18-20, Acts 2:42, John 15:1-17, Titus 2:1-8, John 8:31-32

Setting:

The Testimonial Nowhere.

Cast:

GIRL: A high school girl. Intelligent, but unsure.

Tech needs:

None.

Playwright Notes:

This monologue requires an actor that can be transparent without sounding fake. Much of this monologue is inner thoughts that people seldom articulate. If it helps, the actor can think of herself as vocalizing an internal thought, rather than blathering to a crowd of people.

The beginning of the third paragraph should mark a noticeable change in tone. Through the first two paragraphs, the audience thinks they are seeing a typical church drama where everything works out for the "Christian". Play on that expectation.

This sketch can easily be reworked for a man.

Lights up. GIRL stands center stage.

GIRL: I think I was a pretty average kid. Went to school, hung out with my best friend Leah more often then I cleaned my room, steady B average, not a genius, but not stupid either. Still, I wasn't really happy with my life. It just seemed so...temporary. Then, Amber, one of my other friends, invites Leah and me to her church, and I'm thinking, "No way! People get shunned by going to those places." Still, I wondered what it was like. Leah and I talked about it and eventually agreed to go after the fifth time Amber asked us.

I didn't know what to expect, but the things they said, really made sense. I mean, they really clicked. Their Pastor was awesome and really related well to me, or I to him, or however that works. Anyway, after I had been going for a few weeks, I asked them what it meant to be saved. Leah had the same question. That night, Leah and I got saved then and there. I remember just dancing, madly, to no music whatsoever, we were so happy.

But life didn't get immediately better for me, and in fact, in some ways, it got harder. I knew that there was more to being saved then what I was doing. They told me to read my Bible, and I did, but I couldn't make sense out of it. I wanted to ask questions, but I didn't want to feel stupid. After all, Amber grew up around this stuff, I didn't. My friend Leah started going to this special group, like this Bible study, or whatever, led by this older woman, Diane. Diane was pretty old, like 34, but Leah said she was cool. I couldn't go because I had stuff going on at school.

And that's really where things went different for Leah and me. Leah got really serious about this new faith and it was weird to see how much it changed her. She talked differently, she made new friends. She laughed louder, and cried harder. We didn't like the same movies anymore. Suddenly, for reasons I can't explain, it was really important to her for a guy to be a Christian before she'd date him. A few months passed and I found myself just going through the motions at church, like some sort of holy robot. I didn't want to be fake, but I didn't want to tell them that the fun had worn off either. At the end of the school year, I stopped going altogether. It wasn't benefiting me any, and I didn't see the point in pretending that it did.

Leah's different now than what she was just a few years ago. She's a whole different person. Me? I guess I'm just not like that. I'm the same old me.

Pause.

Honestly, I kinda wish I had gotten to know Diane. I'd be different than I am now, but I think that'd be a good thing.

Yeah, I think it would have been good.

Slow fade to black.

God's Character:

So... What's He like?

Magic Answers

David J. Swanson

The Point:

God is omniscient and the implications of that sometimes have us questioning the things He does.

Biblical Reference:

Deuteronomy 29:29, Romans 11

Setting:

A Park or a school playground.

Cast:

HAROLD-	High school girl. energetic and naïve
ETHYL-	High school girl. energetic and naïve
GERTRUDE-	High school girl. older, wiser, skeptical and sarcastic
DEALER-	Shading looking character. Hat and overcoat.

Tech needs:

Magic 8-ball, Overcoat, Fedora,

Playwright Notes:

This sketch was used to introduce a message on the omnipotence of God. It raises questions about God's nature, but at the same time illustrates how we often have questions beyond what we need to know. The sketch looks like a bad anti-drug skit at first, but quickly descends into the absurd to illustrate our innate demand for answers and the fact that some things we just aren't meant to fully know and understand.

Three high school kids, GERTRUDE, ETHYL, and HAROLD, stand stage left in light-hearted conversation. A surly looking man approaches them with the airs of a drug dealer. He is shifty and overcautious.

DEALER: Psst.

They don't respond.

        Psst.

Nothing.

        Hey you three! Come over here.

GERTRUDE: Who? Us?

DEALER: Yeah, you. Come over here.

They join him center stage.

ETHYL: Who are you?

DEALER: Doesn't matter. I got something for ya.

HAROLD: Um... What do you mean?

DEALER: You three like to have a little fun, right?

ETHYL: I guess so.

DEALER: Well I got something you're gonna love. I've got just the thing you've been looking for.

GERTRUDE: What have we been looking for?

DEALER: Answers, my friend. Answers.

HAROLD: Answers to what?

DEALER: Questions! What else? *(to HAROLD)* You're not too bright, are ya kid?

GERTRUDE: You want to give us answers to our questions?

DEALER: Not me, kid. This!

(He holds up a magic eight ball).

ETHYL: What's that?

DEALER: It's what you've been seeking: Answers to all of life's questions.

HAROLD: Oooooh. It's so mysterious.

GERTRUDE: It's a magic eight ball.

DEALER: It gives you answers.

GERTRUDE: Are they informed answers?

DEALER: They're answers. Wanna try?

HAROLD: Oooh, me first!

(Takes eight ball.)

What do I do?

DEALER: Ask it a question, shake it, and then turn it upside down. You'll have your answer.

HAROLD: I can ask it anything I want?

DEALER: Anything at all.

GERTRUDE: This is stupid.

HAROLD: Um. Will the Giants win the Super Bowl?

(Shakes it, turns it over)

ETHYL: What's it say?

HAROLD: "My sources say no." Dang it.

ETHYL: Oh come on. All the questions in the world and you ask it about the Stupid Bowl? Give me that.

(Takes 8-ball from him)

Will Andrew Johnson ever ask me out?

(Shakes, turns it over, squeals).

"It is decidedly so!" I knew it!

GERTRUDE: It's just a random answer. Don't get your hopes up.

ETHYL: Well you ask it a question then.

GERTRUDE: I don't ask questions of plastic toys.

HAROLD: *(Takes 8-ball back)*

Let me go again. What's a hundred divided by five?

GERTRUDE: It's got to be a yes or no question, otherwise it won't work.

HAROLD: It says "twenty".

GERTRUDE: What?

(Takes it. looks at it.)

Holy cow, it says "twenty".

DEALER: You can ask it anything you want.

Pause as they stand amazed. Then they all grab for it at the same time.

ETHYL: My turn again. Where should I go to college? Butler or Emporia State? (local colleges)

(Turns it over)

"Harvard".

HAROLD: It says Harvard?

ETHYL: It says Harvard. *(To 8-ball)* Why Harvard?

(Turns it over).

It says "Dream big."

HAROLD: Okay, me now.

(Takes 8-ball).

Why won't Julie Pederson talk to me?

(Reads answer to himself)

Oh. Okay, who's next?

ETHYL: What did it say?

HAROLD: Doesn't matter. Who's next?

ETHYL: Tell us what it said.

HAROLD: It said "Halitosis".

All nod in agreement.

GERTRUDE: Yeah, I've been meaning to say something about that.

ETHYL: How does this work, Mister?

DEALER: I can't tell you. But for the right price you can keep it and ask it all of life's most pressing questions.

ETHYL: Can I ask it something more serious?

DEALER: Be my guest.

ETHYL: Why do I feel this pit in my stomach all the time? Like I'm not good enough or something's missing?

(Reads 8-ball. It's clear that it's a long message)

Uh-huh, uh-huh. Oh…

(Hands it to someone else)

GERTRUDE: Care to share?

ETHYL: *(Kind of in a daze)*

Nope. It was for me only. If you want to know, you ask it. I… I need to go home. I need to… *(Exits)*

GERTRUDE: I've got a question for it. Something I've been dying to know.

DEALER: Ask away.

GERTRUDE: If God is all-knowing, then why would he create human beings if He knew that they would sin against him and be cast away from him because He can't be with sinners?

Long pause. Finally,

GERTRUDE: Hmm.

DEALER: What's it say?

GERTRUDE: It says "Good question. Maybe you should ask God."

Blackout

I Don't Buy It

David J. Swanson

The Point:

Is God really a loving God? How do we reconcile the violence and death of the Old Testament with the loving, forgiving God from the New Testament?

Biblical Reference:

Jeremiah 32, Matthew 19

Setting:

The Testimonial Nowhere

Cast:

SARA: Angry, skeptical woman. Any age over 15.

Tech needs:

A Bible.

Playwright Notes:

This is a dangerous script in that it only presents the skeptic's side of the argument. We did this monologue as an introduction to a message on some of the more violent Old Testament stories. It did well to get everyone's attention because you rarely see this kind of questioning given center stage in a worship service. This monologue issues a strong challenge to the speaker to answer these questions. Don't perform this monologue unless you have a strong speaker ready to answer the skeptics and critics.

Sara is angry and speaks with a chip on her shoulder. She's fed up with what she sees as the hypocrisy of God and this is her thesis against it.

SARA: Hi. My name is Sara, and I don't buy it.

I can't buy it. It doesn't make sense. So I don't believe it.

Pause.

You know, they tell you to read your Bible.

"Read your Bible," they say. "Read it every day," they say. But they don't tell you what to do with some of the horrible things that are in it. They don't tell you what to do when God doesn't seem like someone I really want to get to know.

Pause, thinking

Have you read the Old Testament? Have you? Oh sure, everyone loves reading John and Acts and the rest of the New Testament, where God is love, and forgiveness and all that good stuff.

But, what about the Old Testament? What's up with that? Here look, let me give you an example.
(To person in audience)
Can I borrow your Bible? Thanks.
(Takes Bible) I was just reading here yesterday:

She finds Joshua Chapter 6 while she says the next paragraph.

Okay. You remember the story from Sunday School about Joshua and the walls of Jericho? Right? They marched around the city for seven days, then they blew their trumpets and God knocked the walls down. Remember that? Why don't they tell you what happened next? Listen, Joshua 6 verse 20 and 21:

"When the trumpets sounded, the people shouted, and at the sound of the trumpet, when the people gave a loud shout, the wall collapsed; so every man charged straight in, and they took the city. They devoted the city to the LORD and destroyed with the sword every living thing in it—men and women, young and old, cattle, sheep and donkeys."

They killed everything. Why? What's the point of that? What did the donkeys ever do to them? The cattle? They slaughtered all of the children in the whole city, at God's command.

There are others. God tells the Israelites to go into the "promised land" and kill all the people living there. Wake up people! Today they call that "genocide" and it's wrong. It's what the Nazis were trying to do to the Jews, after all. And if it's wrong now, it was wrong 4,000 years ago.

So I don't buy it. I don't buy that God is this loving, forgiving father figure that everyone falls all over themselves to worship. He isn't like that. God has his favorite people, and everyone else…. burns in hell.

Literally.

The God of the Old Testament is the same as the God of the New Testament? I don't buy it.

Blackout

Dueling Detectives

David J. Swanson

The Point:

A creationist looks at the clues of creation and sees God's powerful, creative expressions. An evolutionist looks at the same clues and sees random chance and happenstance. They have the same clues but draw two different conclusions.

The sketch is a discussion on general revelation versus special revelation. Without the special revelation of the Gospel, there are any number of things to which we can attribute the evidences of God. The specific articulation of the Scripture helps us to understand the nature of God in ways that simply observing creation and feeling those longings in our heart cannot.

Biblical Reference:

Romans 1:18-20, Romans 2:14-15, Matthew 28:18-20

Setting:

It is the 1930's in a non-descript big city. A crime scene in a hotel room. There is a bed, a nightstand, a trash can, a suitcase and other hotel amenities. A dead body lies on the floor with chalk or tape around it. The room is disheveled.

Cast:

DETECTIVE HOBBS: New York detective. The younger of the two. Creative, inquisitive, but unable to draw logical conclusions from the evidence at hand.

DETECTIVE SIMPSON: New York detective. The older, wiser detective, though not HOBBS' superior. Easily exasperated by HOBBS.

Tech needs:

If possible, light the scene with orange gels creating a musty, sepia look. Film noir saxophone music introduces the scene but fades into the background fairly quickly. Fake blood on the knife will help to bring some gravitas to the scene.

Playwright Notes:

This sketch demands plenty of props and tech, but the overall effect is worth the effort. Our actors put a lot of work into their dialect to make them sound consistent and believable.

The point of this sketch is well hidden and will be lost without some follow up. If you don't have a speaker addressing this topic, then spend some time introducing the sketch.

As lights come up, film noir-style saxophone music plays. The light is yellowish-orange giving the scene a sepia look.

Detective HOBBS and Detective SIMPSON enter. They each wear trench coats and fedoras and speak with thick New York accents.

SIMPSON: The lieutenant said we'd find the body in here,

(He sees the body lying on the floor)

Ah.

HOBBS: Another day, another dead broad.

SIMPSON: It's enough to get to ya, ain't it, Hobbs.

HOBBS: *(Shrugs)* Eh, it's just the job. Gimme the facts.

SIMPSON: You're gonna love this-

HOBBS: Just the facts, Simpson.

SIMPSON: *(Pulls out notepad.)*

	Police were called here to the Biltmore Hotel at 2:15 this morning. Caller said he'd heard some loud shouting and then what appeared to be the sounds of a struggle emanating from this room.
HOBBS:	Who called?
SIMPSON:	The guy workin' the front desk. His name's Bobby. He's worked here for three months, he's unmarried and he likes to play with Legos.
HOBBS:	I know the type.
SIMPSON:	Yeah, exactly. The cops arrived at 2:35 and, after breaking the door down, found the back window open and the lifeless body of this girl.
	(Kicks at body a little)
	Yep. Dead.
HOBBS:	Got an ID?
SIMPSON:	Yep. The deceased is one Mrs. Ellen Vanderbilt-Donneybrook. Married an ex-con back in January. Rumor was that her family weren't none too happy, neither.
HOBBS:	*(Has wandered over to nightstand.)*
	Whaddya make of this? Two champagne glasses. One with lipstick marks, the other only half drank. I think I see where this night was going.
SIMPSON:	Indeed. Check this out. Looks like someone left their wallet behind.
	(Opens wallet and looks at ID.)
	Yep. Vinnie Donneybrook. It's the vic's husband.
HOBBS:	And what do we have here?
	(Picks up broken heel.)
	Looks like she broke a heel.
SIMPSON:	This one's pretty open and shut if you ask me.

HOBBS: Absolutely.

(Together)

HOBBS: Terrible accident | **SIMPSON:**   Murder One.

Both: What?

SIMPSON: A terrible accident? You're joking right.

HOBBS: You think it was murder? How do you come up with that?

SIMPSON: The girl has three stab wounds in her back, Hobbs.

HOBBS: *(Beat)*

Tragic. Poor girl.

SIMPSON: What exactly do you think happened here?

HOBBS: It's pretty obvious. Look at the evidence. The girl arrived back at her hotel room and discovered, much to her surprise, that she'd mistakenly grabbed her husband's wallet. Upset at her carelessness, she started screaming at herself for her stupidity, which the bellman heard. Then she opened the back window to get some air and poured herself a glass of champagne to calm herself down. Hence the lipstick on the glass. She removed her make-up, obviously getting ready for bed, poured herself a second glass of champagne, no lipstick this time, and then tried to call her husband. Holds up broken heel. However the broken heel can only tell us that the woman clearly hates shoes-

SIMPSON: Hates shoes?

HOBBS: -having stomped on them until the heel broke. In doing so, she dropped the phone and fell backwards and stumbled into a knife that had been carelessly stored sticking out of her luggage.

SIMPSON: *(Sarcasm)* How, unfortunate.

HOBBS: She tried to get up, but fell again, falling on the knife a second time, and then repeated this one more time before succumbing to her injuries. Open and shut case, if you ask me.

SIMPSON: Really? Well then how do you explain this?

(Removes bloody knife from waste basket)

HOBBS: She's very tidy. Just before she died, she put the knife in the trash as she cleaned up. Like I said, terrible accident.

SIMPSON: Well, that's certainly one theory, Hobbs.

HOBBS: Her husband is going to be devastated when he finds out.

SIMPSON: He'll be arrested! Hobbs, he's the perpetrator.

HOBBS: Now where did you come up with that wild idea, Simpson?

SIMPSON: Hobbs! The couple got into an argument. It got violent, a struggle, the man flew into a rage and killed her with a knife from the kitchenette. He panicked when the phone started ringing, took it off the hook so that no one could call, and then fled out the window when the police arrived.

HOBBS: And his wallet?

SIMPSON: He left it behind in a hurry.

HOBBS: How can you be so sure? How can you know that's what happened here?

SIMPSON: Because I read the police report. An eye-witness saw the whole thing. You should try reading up on things.

Blackout

Prayer

A powerful thing...

Prayer Warrior

David J. Swanson

The Point:

> God is all-powerful. Yet sometimes He chooses not to give us what we pray for, even when we're praying selflessly.

Biblical Reference:

> Matthew 6:7, Ecclesiastes 5:2, Zechariah 13:9, John 15:7

Setting:

> A coffee shop.

Cast:

> BETSY: Woman. Teenage to early 30s.
> JOHN: Man. Same age as BETSY.

Tech needs:

> Table, stools, coffee cups, working cell phone.

Playwright Notes:

> This simple and short sketch gets right to the point. Sometimes we're disappointed in the way that God answers our prayers. This opens up the discussion for the speaker. The actress playing the last line needs lots of time to listen to the tale and to break down. She needs to go from quietly confident that God will answer her prayer, to distraught and confused. She only has a few lines while on the phone, so give her plenty of time.

Lights up. BETSY is sitting at a coffee table in a coffee shop. She is on her cell phone.

BETSY: *(On the phone.)* That's what Dad said…. Yeah.

JOHN, a friend of BETSY's enters and sees BETSY. It's a chance encounter and both wave to each other quietly while BETSY continues her phone call.

BETSY: *(On the phone)* Well, we're all praying for her…. Okay, thanks for calling. *(Hangs up phone).* Hey, John.

JOHN: Hi Betsy. How are you?

BETSY: Eh, I've been better. It's been a rough week.

JOHN: How so?

BETSY: *(Indicates phone)* Oh, that was my Aunt Robin from Connecticut.. My grandma isn't doing so well.

JOHN: Your mom's mom?

BETSY: No, my dad's mom. She lives in Connecticut.

JOHN: What's wrong?

BETSY: She went in to the hospital last Saturday.

JOHN: Oh no. I'm sorry, I didn't hear. What happened?

BETSY: She was feeling a little dizzy a few weeks ago, and last Saturday she fell and completely passed out. Grandpa said she was out for something like ten minutes. Anyway, my grandpa took her to the hospital and they did a bunch of tests. They're not sure exactly what it is but it's either a brain tumor or cancer on her brain.

JOHN: I'm so sorry. What can they do for her?

BETSY: Well, the doctors say at her age it's a pretty slim chance of surviving it. Apparently whatever is causing this has been there for a while.

JOHN: So are you going out to see her?

BETSY:	My Dad is out there now. At this point, there isn't much point in me going out there. I can't do anything for her.
JOHN:	Well, there is one thing you can do.
BETSY:	Pray?
JOHN:	Exactly.
BETSY:	Just turn it all over to God.
JOHN:	He's all powerful. The Bible says that anything you ask in His name, He'll do for you.
BETSY:	I know. We've been praying like maniacs. The doctors say there's almost no chance that she'll make it through this, but they don't know our God.
JOHN:	*(Stands to leave)*. Hey, He created the universe. He can get rid of a little tumor. So can I pray for you and your family too?
BETSY:	Please do. The more the better.
JOHN:	Hey I've got to get going. But I'll be praying that our all-powerful God cures your grandma.
BETSY:	Thanks.

JOHN leaves.

BETSY:	*(Her phone rings. Answers cell phone)*.
	Hello? Hi Aunt Robin.
	(Pause grows increasingly upset).
	When?
	(Long pause while she listens. Her grandmother has died.)
	But I don't understand. We prayed…. I prayed…

Blackout

Three Different Prayers

David J. Swanson

The Point:

When Moses was outside the Camp in prayer, he went away to meet with God. He called it the "place of meeting." And he talked with God. It was a two way discussion and it was transparent and honest. Our prayer lives have to reflect that two-way honesty that God had with Moses. Prayer is essential in our discipline and growth.

Biblical Reference:

Exodus 33, Romans 8:26-27, Matthew 26:39

Setting:

Each actor is in a different scene but all are praying before bedtime. One could be kneeling, one sitting, and one pacing.

Cast:

ACTOR 1:   A teenager or 20 something. She Is angry with God. God has not answered her prayers and now demands answers. While she is angry, it is still an honest two-way conversation.

ACTOR 2:   A graduating senior looking to go to college. He prays fervently, though he is in a good place. He is asking God for guidance on his future.

ACTOR 3:   A teenager who prays automatically without thinking. He has a laundry list and he says many of these things every night with the exact same tone, word for word.

Tech needs:

The scene should be lit with soft blue light for evening. Each character is in a different setting, though they don't necessarily need separate pools of light. Sound effects of crickets chirping can help set the mood.

Playwright Notes:

The juxtaposition of these three prayers highlights the banality of our prayer life. You'll find the audience laughing when Actor 3 prays for his football team to win following Actor 1's lament over cancer. The perspective change is convicting and gently reminds us to take everything to God in prayer but in a real way.

Lights up.

ACTOR 3: *(Distracted. Praying automatically)*

Dear God. Thank you that school went well today. I pray that it goes good tomorrow. Thank you for my family. Thank you for all the good things you put in my life.

ACTOR 2: *(As if talking to a close friend)*

Father God, thank you for being such a loving, powerful God. Lord, my life is really exciting right now. In a lot of ways, I wonder if this is as good as it's going to get.

ACTOR 1: *(Upset)*

Father God. I am so angry with you right now. I know I shouldn't be, but I am. Why are you doing this to me? Where are you? Why aren't you doing anything?

ACTOR 2: School is awesome right now. I love my teachers, well, most of my teachers. Mr. Granderson is still a pain, but he's okay, I guess. My volleyball team is winning, and my parents haven't been fighting much lately. I wanted to say thank you, God. Thank you for giving me these blessings.

ACTOR 1: I don't know how often I've been right here, on my knees, begging you to step in. You're the most powerful God in the universe. Why can't you use a little power here? For me? Aren't I worth a small portion of your infinite power?

ACTOR 3: God, I pray that I'll make the football team, at least third string. I don't want to play JV again. I pray that I pass my calc test, even though I didn't study. I pray that Brett gets the new Call of Duty game so we can play at his house.

ACTOR 2: But Father, it's time I start deciding what I'm going to do for college. This is a huge decision, God, and I don't want to make it without Your wisdom. I've always had my heart set on KU. A big school. It's a real college town with the real college experience. So much happens there. There are so many opportunities. But Dad says it costs too much. He thinks I should do junior college first and save some money.

ACTOR 1: *(Begins softly but builds in energy through the end of the line)* Mom isn't getting any better. Dad keeps smiling and telling me that she'll be alright, but he's always been a bad liar. I can see it in his eyes, hear it in his voice. Mom won't be here for Christmas. She won't be here for when I go to prom, or when I go off to college. She won't be there when I get married. How is that fair, God? Why won't you stop this cancer?

(Beat)

ACTOR 3: I pray that the Chiefs win this week, that I don't forget my orthodontist appointment again, and that mom packs those pudding cups I like for lunch. Please, help me to wake up on time for school tomorrow.

ACTOR 2: God please give me the wisdom and the opportunity to decide what to do. I know ultimately it's not what Dad wants and it's not what I want. It's what you want Father.

ACTOR 1: God, I don't understand. Won't you please help her? Can't you help my mom?

ACTOR 2:   Help me, to discern what you want for me.

ACTOR 3:   And if you can work it that I sit next to Penny Harding in study hall, that would be cool too. Thank you, God. Amen

ACTOR 2:   Amen.

ACTOR 1:   *(Whispered)* Amen.

Slow fade to black.

Reaching Out

What about the others?

For Want of a Sandwich

David J. Swanson

The Point:

You can't ignore someone's physical needs and only minister to their spiritual needs. When we reach out to others through their immediate needs we'll find we've built a relationship and they'll be much more likely to listen to anything else we have to say. For want of a sandwich, an opportunity to share the gospel was lost.

Biblical Reference:

Acts 20:35, John 13:12-14, Mark 10:44-45

Setting:

A bench at a bus stop.

Cast:

JOSH: Bum. Hungry.
DUFFY: Self absorbed teenage girl.
ADELE: Self absorbed teenage girl.
JASON: Man in his 20s.
TED: All of the negative stereotypes of a "bible thumper".
GREG: 20s or 30s man. Careful to notice when someone is in need.

Tech needs:

A park bench. Sound effects of traffic, bus arriving and departing. A lunch bag with chips and a sandwich in it.

Playwright Notes:

Josh must be long suffering. His hunger is an all consuming thought for him, yet it does not cause him to lash out or speak sarcastically. The last encounter with Greg should be soft and sweet. A relationship is built through the sharing of the food, though sadly, this person does not have the gospel to share.

Sound effect of a busy intersection.

Lights up. A bum, JOSH, lies down on a bench at a bus stop.

DUFFY and ADELE enter in mid conversation.

DUFFY: So I said to him, I said Edward, we can't go on like this.

ADELE: You said that.

DUFFY: I did. Oh, was he mad.

ADELE: Now is this before or after you realized he was a vampire?

DUFFY: Very funny. But anyway- *(Notices JOSH on bench)*

ADELE: What?

DUFFY: Oh. Do you see that man?

ADELE: Yes.

DUFFY: He's one of those people.

ADELE: What do you mean?

DUFFY: Homeless.

ADELE: Ew.

DUFFY: I know.

ADELE: Where does he sleep?

DUFFY: Here, I suppose.

ADELE: Ugh. He probably smells.

DUFFY: Yes, let's not get too close.

ADELE: We might catch poor.

DUFFY: I've heard it's contagious.

JOSH: I can hear you, you know.

DUFFY: Oh, geez. He's awake. Sorry! Thought you were sleeping.

JOSH: *(Sits up).*

Do you have any food?

Sound effect of bus arriving.

ADELE: Um. Here's our bus.

JOSH: I'd like a sandwich.

DUFFY: We'll be praying for you…. whoever you are. God is good!

They exit. JASON enters.

JASON: Excuse me… excuse me. Old man.

JOSH: I'm not old.

JASON: I'm sorry. I was just wondering if this was the bus to Northford.

JOSH: Twenty-seven.

JASON: Sorry?

JOSH: You said I was old. I'm twenty-seven.

JASON: I didn't know. I'm just trying to get to Northford.

JOSH: You might have asked.

JASON: Look, I need to get to Northford.

JOSH: I have no idea.

JASON: A lot of help you are.

JOSH: I'm hungry…

JASON Exits. TED enters.

TED: Repent! Repent in the name of Christ! Repent!

JOSH: Not so loud, I'm trying to sleep.

TED: And I am trying to preach the word, my good man. What's your name, friend?

Sits up at this new human interaction.

JOSH: Josh.

TED: Well, Josh, today is the day that's going to change your life. You know what you are?

JOSH: Hungry.

TED: Lost. You're lost, Josh. But you know what I have for you?

JOSH: Food?

TED: No sir. The good news. I'm here to tell you the good news. Here, can you see this?

JOSH: Is it a sandwich?

TED: No, sir, it's a Bible. The Word of the Lord.

JOSH: It looks like a sandwich. Can I eat it?

TED: No Josh, you can't. It's better than a sandwich. It's the bread of life.

JOSH: What kind of bread, did you say?

TED: Living water, my friend.

JOSH: I thought you said it was bread.

TED: The well where life springs eternal. The Word of God.

JOSH: Maybe a little bite?

TED: Josh, you can't eat my Bible, okay? Now are you going to listen or not?

Pause.

JOSH: I'm sorry, what did you say? I think my body is trying to digest itself.

TED: Ugh. Look, I want to share the good news with you, but I'm not going to force it down your throat.

JOSH: You could force a sandwich down my throat.

TED: I'm sorry Josh. I can't waste time with you. There are those that are hungry for the Word. I must seek them out.

TED exits

JOSH: I'm hungry....

GREG enters carrying a lunch pail.

GREG: Hey.

JOSH: Hi.

GREG:	What's your name?
	(sits on bench next to JOSH)
JOSH:	I'm Josh.
GREG:	Hi, I'm Greg. Nice to meet you.
JOSH:	Eh.
GREG:	Hey, I've got an extra bag of chips in here. You want it?
JOSH:	Really?
GREG:	Yeah. I've got a sandwich in here too if you want it.

Takes sandwich. Looks at GREG with appreciation and then puts his head on GREG's shoulder.

JOSH:	You're not one of those Christians, are you?
GREG:	Who me? Nah. Couldn't stomach much of religion. I'm just a guy getting by.
JOSH:	Why are you doing this?
GREG:	Doing what?
JOSH:	Being so nice to me? Giving me food?
GREG:	Well, you're hungry, ain't ya?

JOSH Nods head vehemently.

Well, it's just not right to let another person go hungry. It's called being a decent human being, the way I see it.

Pause. JOSH considers GREG for a few beats, then finally relaxes.

JOSH:	Thank you.

Blackout

Coins or the Pile

David J. Swanson

The Point:

My home church has been given the vision of planting or daughtering churches until our county is saturated with Bible believing churches that passionately pursue Christ. This sketch serves as a visual illustration that ultimately, it's about reaching out to those in the community.

Biblical Reference:

Matthew 28:18-19

Setting:

A non-descript bare stage. The stage is covered with hundreds (if not thousands) of coins. We used large plastic pirate coins since they were shiny and easy to see. They litter the stage completely from end to end, back to front.

Cast:

MR. EDWARDS: The manager of a large bank.
WENDY: A new employee.
SAL, BILL, HILLARY, JENNIFER, JAMIE, JAMIE, SEAN, ROBERTA, TAMI:
                  Additional characters, any age.

Tech Needs:

Many coins. If mics are needed, mic MR. EDWARDS and WENDY and then mic the stage with a floor mic to pick up the rest.

Playwright Notes:

Typically, if you're witnessing a cheesy Christian drama, you'll find that it is a confusing mix of allegory and melodrama. Of all of the sketches in this book, this one comes closest to that definition. We have a metaphor of picking up coins to represent spreading the gospel, and then we have an excess of absurd behavior driving the action.

However, this sketch succeeds because it plays off of the audience's expectations. Just when the audience expects the next character to walk on and point out how silly things are, they join the pile and prolong the absurdity. No one expects a pile of 10 actors on stage, even in the largest church drama groups.

The goal of this sketch is to provide a vivid picture of the absurdity of Christians piling into a church hoping to reach the lost. Play on that absurdity as much as possible. This one is not about character studies and deep subtext, but rather using the ridiculousness to get a visceral reaction from the audience.

This is also a great sketch for getting new actors on stage with minimal pressure. They can get used to rehearsals, being under the lights and in front of people, without having more than a few lines.

MR. EDWARDS and WENDY enter stage right. They walk slowly. MR. EDWARDS is showing WENDY around the company for the first time.

MR. EDWARDS: Wendy, I couldn't be happier that you've decided to work for us.

WENDY: Thank you, sir.

MR. EDWARDS: I have a very important job for you, Wendy. Do you see all of these coins?

WENDY: Yes sir. I was going to ask about that.

MR. EDWARDS: I need you to pick them up.

WENDY: Are they particularly valuable?

MR. EDWARDS: Extremely. If one of them were to go missing, I would drop everything just to find the one that was lost.

WENDY: I see.

MR. EDWARDS: So, here are some bags. Bring the coins up to the accountant when you've got them cleaned up. Can you do that?

WENDY: Yes, sir!

MR. EDWARDS exits. WENDY looks around, decides on a place to start, and kneels downstage left. She picks up a coin, looks at it and puts it in a bag. WENDY sits back satisfied for a second before looking for the next coin to pick up. SAL enters.

SAL: Whoa, look at this mess!

WENDY: Tell me about it.

SAL: Want some help?

WENDY: Sure! I mean, if you don't mind.

SAL: Not at all.

(SAL gets down on hands and knees immediately next to WENDY)

Which one should we pick up first?

WENDY: *(Points at a coin)*

How about this one?

SAL: All right.

Together, they both pick up a single coin and then put it in the bag. They do this two more times. They move slower than WENDY doing it by herself.

WENDY: Thanks for the help. They don't seem as heavy with your help.

BILL enters.

BILL: Whatcha doing?

SAL: Picking up coins.

BILL: Can I help?

WENDY: Sure.

BILL kneels immediately next to them and the three pick up a single coin together and put it in the bag together.

BILL:	This is fun.
SAL:	Isn't it?
BILL:	It feels good to give back, ya know?
SAL:	How many do we have so far?
WENDY:	Four.

HILLARY and JENNIFER enter.

HILLARY:	What are you guys doing?

This is said as if they realize how stupid it is for three people to pick up a single coin. The audience thinks this is where the sketch will turn.

WENDY:	Picking up coins. Wanna help?
JENNIFER:	Sure!

HILLARY jumps in next to them. JENNIFER can't figure out where to kneel and eventually piles on top of the four kneeling people. The group of five pick up one coin together and put it in the bag. They pick up another coin and put it in the bag. They move painfully slowly.

BILL:	How many do we have?
WENDY:	Six!
SAL:	Woohoo!

JAMIE, SEAN, and JAMIE enter

JAMIE:	Hey, that looks fun. Can we join you?
HILLARY:	Absolutely.

They jump on top. The four on the bottom collapse and now it's a huge dog pile. Improv - oof, ow, my leg. I can't move, etc. They no longer can pick up the coins as a pile.

SEAN:	So, what are we doing here?
JENNIFER:	Picking up coins.
JAMIE:	Ah coins. Good idea. How many do we have?
WENDY:	SIX!

SEAN:	It feels so good to be a part of something so big.
HILLARY:	I know. Look at the size of this pile!

TAMI and ROBERTA enter.

ROBERTA:	What on earth is going on here?
SEAN:	We made a pile! Wanna join?
TAMI:	Are you kidding? Of course!

ROBERTA and TAMI pile on top. Loud groans from the pile.

WENDY:	Are you guys even picking up coins up there?
ROBERTA:	Coins?
WENDY:	Yeah, we're supposed to be picking up coins.
ROBERTA:	*(ROBERTA is laying face up on the pile in complete relaxation.)* To be honest, I'm not really around any coins. You guys on the ground are in a better position. However, you have my full support.
SAL:	I can't move my arm to even reach the coins. Look at how many we have left to pick up!
BILL:	You know what would be better?
SAL:	What?
BILL:	If the coins came to us.

They think for a while.

SAL:	Here, penny, penny, penny!
BILL:	Are they coming?
SAL:	Nope.
HILLARY:	Wait! I have an idea!
	(Everyone drops silent)
	Let's go to them!
WENDY:	Brilliant!

The entire pile attempts to move. They slowly work their way towards center stage. They may not even move, just try to move.

TAMI: Well this is stupid.

                    (Gets off of pile and moves downstage right)

ROBERTA: What are you doing?

TAMI: If we're supposed to pick up coins, I'm going to start over here.

ROBERTA: But won't you miss the pile? It's warm and comfy...

SAL: *(Feeling crushed at the bottom of the pile)*

                    Not so comfy!

TAMI picks up several coins and puts them in a bag. This blows WENDY's mind.

WENDY: Whoa! What on earth? Look at her! How many coins do you
                    have already?

TAMI: Seven.

WENDY: SEVEN?! We've only got six.

BILL: She's a genius! We should go over there!

Improv- yeah! Much better idea! ROBERTA, HILLARY, JENNIFER, SEAN, JAMIE, JAMIE, BILL and finally SAL, get off the first pile and pile on top of TAMI. (oof! Ow!)

WENDY: *(Stands)*

                    Wait, wait, wait, wait! This is stupid.

                    (The idea comes to him very slowly)

                    What if.... What if we all, like, we all... spread out?

Silence.

ROBERTA: But... what about the pile?

WENDY: *(Sincerely)*

                    I don't think it's about the pile. It's about the coins.

They concede that it's worth a shot. Everyone spreads out into groups of 2 or 3 (representing small churches). Together they stoop down and gather up the coins around them. They begin slowly but the more coins they get, the more excited they get. Soon, all of the coins on stage are picked up. This should take 5-10 seconds. They are shocked and exhilarated by their own productivity. The remainder of the sketch is a rolling crescendo of excitement culminating in WENDY's final line.

SEAN: I can't believe it! Look at how many coins we've got.

JAMIE: Ooh! I see more over there!
(Runs off Far Right aisle)

SEAN: I see them! Wait!
(Runs off behind JAMIE)

JAMIE: And there!
(Runs through RC aisle)

ROBERTA: There's more this way!
(Runs off Center aisle)

TAMI: Let's keep going!
(Runs off LC aisle)

JENNIFER: Why stop now?
(Runs of far left aisle)

HILLARY: This way! *(Exits)*

SAL: Out the doors! *(Exits)*

BILL: Into the streets! *(Exits)*

WENDY: And to the ends of the earth! *(ECCxits)*

Blackout

Christmas

It's beginning to look a lot like...

Down to Earth

David J. Swanson

The Point:

> When Jesus came down to earth, He left a perfect home in heaven where he sat at the right hand of God. He left all of that for us, even though we'd rejected him. His love for us is greater than we'll ever appreciate.

Biblical Reference:

> Luke 2, Isaiah 9:6, John 1:14, Hebrews 2:9, Ephesians 1:5

Setting:

> Modern day working environments. Scene 1 is a large corporate executive office. Scene 2 is a cramped mail room and Scene 3 is a small office as would befit a junior sales executive.

Cast:

> JAMES: Middle aged man. High level manager. Recently divorced. JAMES is allegorically Christ, though he is not meant to actually be Christ.
>
> GABE: Young professional just out of college.
>
> KATHERINE: JAMES' ex-wife. She harbors pent up hostility brought on by living a selfish life and living apart from God. She's justified her actions to herself but gets angry when her justifications are exposed.

Tech needs:

> Lights should isolate each scene if you have multiple sets. A mailroom needs a sorting table and a mail chute. You can be as ambitious or as simple as you want with set and props but make sure there's enough stuff with which the actors can interact.

Playwright Notes:

> We performed this three scene short play as part of our Christmas Eve service a few years ago. It is ambitious and ended up being deeply impactful to those who saw it. Instead of running all of the

scenes and then having our pastor speak, we allowed the speaker to speak in between scenes to help draw out the allegory we were trying to create.

When we performed this, instead of a blackout at each scene, we dimmed the lights halfway and had the actors freeze. It gave the audience a visual to consider while the pastor spoke. Of course, at some point you have to go to full blackout and let your actor get ready for the next scene.

This play doesn't necessarily have to be set at Christmas time. You can easily remove the Christmas Eve references and set it at any time of year. It works at Christmas Eve when you're talking about Christ coming to Earth, but it could be performed any time of year.

SCENE 1

A large office. This is the office of a director or upper level manager. It is well appointed and spacious. A large desk and chair dominate the center with additional seating on the other side of the desk. Boxes are strewn about, half filed with file folders and books. The look of the office is one of transition, either moving into or out of the office.

JAMES wears an expensive looking suit. GABE a button-down shirt but no tie.

It is the first day of work after Thanksgiving. The Christmas season has started. JAMES sits in the chair facing away from the door. He stares transfixed at a photo frame in his hand.

GABE knocks outside JAMES' door even though it is open. At first JAMES does not respond. GABE knocks again. GABE is clearly nervous.

JAMES: Come.

GABE: Good morning, Mr. Anderson. Did you have a good Thanksgiving?

JAMES: Mmm.

GABE: Christmas season is officially in full swing. I love this time of year.

(Awkward pause as JAMES ignores him).

Er, anyway I was told to run these quarterly reports up to you since you wanted to see them.

JAMES: *(Distracted)*

Eh. Put them on my desk.

(Turns to GABE)

Thank you….uh….

GABE: Rodgers, sir. Gabe Rogers.

JAMES: Yes, Gabe, of course. Sorry. My mind is elsewhere.

GABE: That's alright. A person in your position can't be expected to know every single person who works for him.

JAMES: Not at all. Your name just slipped my mind.

GABE: *(Sees boxes)*

Sir, are you moving to a new office?

JAMES: I guess you could say that.

GABE: Is there a better office in the building than the corner office?

JAMES: Not exactly, Gabe.

(Beat)

I'm taking a new job.

GABE: They're moving you to vice president already? Congratulations, sir!

JAMES:	No, Gabe. I'm leaving the company.
	(Pause as GABE is speechless)
	You might as well know now. The company will be sending out an email this afternoon.
GABE:	I can't believe it, sir. After all you've done for the company, and they just treat you like that. They just throw you out like yesterday's garbage? It's despicable. It's unethical. It's-.
JAMES:	It's my choice to leave, Gabe.
GABE:	Oh... right.
	(Pause)
	But sir, you'll miss out on your Christmas bonus.
JAMES:	I'm not worried about that right now.
GABE:	If you don't mind me asking, sir, why are you leaving?
JAMES:	It's because of my wife.
GABE:	She didn't like the long hours? Wants you home for dinner, I imagine...
JAMES:	No. She left me. She moved out four months ago. She's technically my ex-wife, though I mean to do something about that.
GABE:	So... what'd you do?
JAMES:	I beg your pardon.
GABE:	-to make her leave?
JAMES:	Would you ask me something like this if I wasn't leaving the company?
GABE:	Absolutely not. Honestly, I was terrified of you until you told me you were quitting. Now, you're... just another guy. So...?
JAMES:	Just another guy.... Fine. You want to talk man to man? We can do that.
GABE:	Lay it on me, James. Can I call you James?

JAMES: No.

GABE: Jimmy? Jimbo?

(Pause. Then sits in chair, making himself comfortable)

Alright, Mr. Anderson. I'm listening.

JAMES: A little over a year ago I found some emails on my wife's computer that I obviously wasn't supposed to find. They were letters of an amorous nature and they were not addressed to me. It was a week before our tenth anniversary. I confronted her about the relationship, which of course, she denied. I found some texts on her phone and finally she admitted to having an affair.

We started going to a counselor, but it was obvious that my wife was just putting in her time. Four months ago, I found out that she had never broken it off with the other guy. I told her she was to end it with him for good. She could not be married to two men. She could not love and respect me while he was in the picture.

She told me she needed a day to think about it.

The next day I came home to find a manila envelope on the kitchen counter. Inside was a letter saying that I'd forced her to do this. She had divorce papers already made up. Apparently she was just waiting for the right time to give them to me. She withdrew nearly all of our savings, took her jewelry, and not much else before she left.

	According to the judge, my wife's paperwork "alleged incompatibility", whatever that means. He granted the divorce despite my wishes.
GABE:	I'm so sorry Mr. Anderson. I had no idea you'd gone through all that.
JAMES:	Most people didn't. Work has a wonderful way of burying our personal failures.
GABE:	So is this a fresh start then? You're leaving the company to start over somewhere else.
JAMES:	I'm going after her, Gabe.
GABE:	What? Why?
	(The way he says "why" implies, "why would you go after someone like that?") I mean, no offense-.
JAMES:	I don't expect you to understand. I found out that she got a job as a sales rep at a marketing firm in California. I'm selling the house and taking a job at her firm.
GABE:	But why quit your job to go after her, after all she did to you?
JAMES:	Because I chose her. I chose her to be my wife, perfect or not. For better or worse, she's the one I choose to love.
GABE:	You can't force someone to love you, sir.
JAMES:	No. But I can choose to love her regardless of how she treats me.
GABE:	You're giving up an awful lot just to be with her.
JAMES:	I'd give up everything to be with her.

Blackout

Optional Interlude

A speaker discusses the truth that Jesus was in a pretty high authority in heaven above. He talks through Isaiah 6 and talks about where Jesus came from, and the sacrifice of leaving normalcy might have been for Jesus.

SCENE 2

JAMES is in a mail room with a mail chute and mail sorting rack. Large piles of mail surround him. He is dirty and obviously worn out. He wears worn clothes and looks unkempt.

Lights up. Sound effect – mail sorting machines.

JAMES is on the phone and is speaking animatedly. He is wearing dirty, work clothes, possibly threadbare.

JAMES: I'm terribly sorry Mr. Adams…. Yes, I know that accounts receivable is on the third floor. They must have been sorted incorrectly. We've been overloaded with the Christmas mail crush this week…. Yes, sir. I'll be right up to take the mail to the correct floor. ….I know, I'm sorry sir… No, I have no idea if any of your Christmas cards went to the wrong floor. I'm sorry… Yes sir, I'll do better in the future.

(He hangs up. He sorts a few more letters from a sack before praying.)

(JAMES' attitude changes to one of resignation, frustration, and despondency. It should have a Garden of Gethsemane feel to it.)

If this is some sort of test, God, I wonder if I'm passing it.

"Go", you said. "Go after her". I heard you as clear as day. I should have asked "at what cost"? Then again, maybe it's better that I didn't.

All of my friends think I'm crazy, God. Well, what friends I have left. They call it a fool's errand. They say it's foolish to give up a six figure salary, my position, my career, my house, everything. They say she made her choice. "Why lower yourself to her level?" they ask.

I've been here a month, Lord. How much longer must I endure the ridicule, the insults, and the $8 an hour that barely pays for the gas to get here? For what? For the privilege of sorting the mail of kids ten years younger than me with all of the politeness of half-starved animals. Ooh, if they only knew how I was respected back home. If they only knew-

(Pause)

Yet, still… If given the chance to leave and have my old job back, my old life back, the truth is, I wouldn't take it. I love her, Lord. I love her more than anything in this world. You know that.

I guess that's why you sent me here. You love her too.

Blackout

Optional Interlude

Talk about the movement of Christ from Glory to this earth using John 1:14 or Philippians 2 or Isaiah 53. He dwelt among us. There were times when he looked around at humanity and declared his unbelievable love for the humanity that he was amongst. This kept him moving forward towards the cross.

SCENE 3

A small office. KATHERINE is busily typing on her computer. The office is tastefully decorated for Christmas.

JAMES enters through the open door. He does not knock, she does not look at him as he enters.

JAMES: Working awfully hard on a Christmas Eve, aren't you?

She looks up and freezes in disbelief.

KATHERINE: What are you doing here?

JAMES: I'm delivering mail. Christmas cards, by the looks of it.

KATHERINE: I'm not kidding, James. (Crosses and closes the door) Why are you here?

JAMES: This is my job.

KATHERINE: You work here?

JAMES: I do.

KATHERINE: I don't have time for games.

JAMES: I'm not playing.

KATHERINE: I took this job and moved out here to make it easier on both of us.

JAMES: No you didn't. You left to make it easier for yourself. I never wanted you to leave.

KATHERINE: You're 2000 miles from home.

JAMES: As are you.

KATHERINE: Go home James.

JAMES: Not without my wife.

KATHERINE: *(Getting animated.)* I'm not your wife anymore. Or did you not hear the judge clearly?

JAMES: I never wanted to divorce you.

KATHERINE: You signed the papers.

JAMES: I had to. You forced my hand, Katherine. You wanted your freedom.

KATHERINE: And so you fly out and pretend to work here?

JAMES: I'm not pretending, Katherine. I work here now.

Silence. KATHERINE softens as she processes the possibility that he actually works there.

KATHERINE: What about your regional manager job? That was your dream job.

JAMES: I quit.

KATHERINE: You quit?

JAMES: Yeah, it was my dream job, but I wasn't living my dream life. My dream life was living with you. Waking up to you every morning.

KATHERINE: Fighting every morning, you mean.

JAMES: I miss that.

KATHERINE: You miss that?

JAMES: Yeah. It was when we stopped fighting that I knew that we were in trouble.

Pause.

KATHERINE: So what, you're some sort of clerk now?

JAMES: Mailroom. It's not exactly the right economy to be moving jobs.

KATHERINE: Where are you living?

JAMES: Do you remember my friend Randy, from college. He lives out here. I get to crash on his couch, and we have all the Ramen noodle we could ever need.

KATHERINE: You're sleeping on Randy's couch?   For what?

JAMES: For you.

KATHERINE: Stop it.

JAMES: I won't.

KATHERINE: James, don't you think I know I'm a horrible person? You have to show up here and prove your point? I know I was terrible to you. I know I caused our divorce. You don't have to show up here like a perfect little angel to tell me how awful I am.

JAMES: That's not why I came. That's not the Katherine I remember.

KATHERINE: Well, you have some short memory.

JAMES: I remember you as my beautiful bride. I remember you as the perfect match for me.

Pause.

KATHERINE: You haven't asked me about him yet?

JAMES: I wasn't going to.

KATHERINE: Well if you must know, we're not together anymore. It didn't work out.

JAMES: I didn't ask.

KATHERINE: Things weren't any better with him than they were with you.

JAMES: I don't care.

KATHERINE: It turns out that I'm the problem.

    (Pause)

Why are you here James?

JAMES: I'm here because I love you.

KATHERINE: *(She starts to cry)* Don't say that. Don't say that!

JAMES: But it's true.

KATHERINE: You can't love me. The way I've hurt you, the problems…. I'm a mess. You can't love me.

JAMES: I love you, Katherine.

They exchange a glance. KATHERINE can't bear his gaze.

KATHERINE: You're insane. We had our shot. It didn't work.

JAMES: I'm not giving up on you, Katherine. I'm here to make it work.

KATHERINE: I'm sorry, James. It's impossible…. It's just… impossible.

Slow fade to black.

Optional Concluding Remarks and Invitation

Talk about how God pursued us initially here on this earth coming as a little baby, even though we had "divorced" ourselves from him. Present the amazing plan of salvation.

Made in the USA
Middletown, DE
03 April 2015